THE GRACE BIBLE

1–2 PETER

PAUL ELLIS

The Grace Bible: 1–2 Peter

ISBN: 978-1-927230-79-4

Published by KingsPress, P.O. Box 66145, Beach Haven 0749, New Zealand. Visit www.kingspress.org for information.

This title is part of a series and is available in other formats. Visit thegracebible.com for information.

Please note that KingsPress' publishing style capitalizes certain pronouns in Scripture that refer to the Father, Son, and Holy Spirit, and may differ from some publisher's styles.

Version: 1.0 (March 2023)

Contents

What is The Grace Bible?

> My only aim is to complete the task the Lord Jesus has given me – the task of testifying to the good news of God's grace. (Acts 20:24)

The good news of God's grace declares that God is not mad at you, he's mad about you. The One who sits on a throne of grace blesses you, not because you are good, but because he is good and he longs to be good to you.

Grace declares that God is for us and with us, and he freely gives us everything we need for life and godliness. Grace invites you to come in from the cold, rest from your labors, and feast at the table of his abundance. Grace is what makes the new covenant new and the good news *good news*.

If you have ever asked, "How do I read this scripture through a new covenant lens?" *The Grace Bible* is for you.

This book is not a law Bible with rules to follow, nor is it a works Bible that tells you what to do. It is not a judgment Bible to fear, or a guilt Bible to make you feel bad. It is a *grace* Bible that reveals the good news found on every page of scripture.

In this study Bible, you will find no guilt or condemnation and none of the usual calls for blood, sweat, and tears. Our focus will be on Jesus Christ—who he is, what he has done, and what you can do because of what he has done.

The Grace Bible is for the weary and those tired of pretending. It's for the burned out, the fed up, and the knocked down. It's for those who are in distress, or debt, or are discontented.

It's for all of us who need grace.

Keywords of Grace from 1–2 Peter

> May grace and peace be yours in the fullest measure.
> (1 Peter 1:2)

The gospel of grace proclaims the unconditional love of the Father, the complete forgiveness of sins, and the gracious provision of all the blessings of heaven that are ours in Christ. In contrast with the old covenant emphasis on self-improvement and rule-keeping, the primary takeaway of the new covenant is to believe in Jesus, the Son of God, who died and rose again. We are exhorted to grow in the grace and knowledge of his love and live in such a way that others will glorify God and be drawn into the orbit of his love.

To what extent are these themes present in Peter's two epistles? We can answer this question by identifying his keywords of grace.

Believe/believers. The chief takeaway of the new covenant is to believe in the Lord Jesus Christ, and this exhortation is echoed by Peter (1 Pet. 1:8). We come to God the Father through faith in Jesus his Son (1 Pet. 1:21). Those who believe in the Lord will never be disappointed (1 Pet. 2:6).

Born again. The believer has been born again or begotten by God (1 Pet. 1:3). Because you have been born of imperishable seed, the living and enduring word of God, you are eternally saved and eternally secure (1 Pet. 1:23).

Cross, The. On the cross, the Son of God dealt with our sins once and for all so that we might be reconciled to God (1 Pet. 3:18). His sacrifice means we can live free and whole (1 Pet. 2:24), with souls that have been purified from all sin (1 Pet. 1:22, 2 Pet. 1:9).

Faith. Peter distinguishes different kinds of faith. Saving faith, such as the apostles had, is based on the gift of Christ's righteousness (2 Pet. 1:1). Our faith is not in ourselves, but in God, who raised Christ from the dead (1 Pet. 1:21). Our God-given faith is more precious than gold for it sustains us in our trials (1 Pet. 1:7), is the foundation of all spiritual growth (2 Pet. 1:5), and is the means by which we receive the salvation of our souls (1 Pet. 1:9).

Father. In the old covenant, God was seen as an aloof judge recording all your sins. But in the new covenant the apostles reveal a God who cares for you like a Father (1 Pet. 1:2, 5:7). Peter encourages us to call God "Father" (1 Pet. 1:17), and he refers to believers as the children (1 Pet. 1:14), household (1 Pet. 4:17), and people of God (1 Pet. 2:10).

Forgiveness. The gospel that Peter preaches proclaims that Christ died for sins once for all (1 Pet. 3:18). All our sins – past, present, and future – were dealt with at the cross once and for all time. Those who believe this good news have their souls purified (1 Pet. 1:22).

Good deeds. Doing good and doing right are themes that echo through Peter's first epistle (see 1 Pet. 1:15, 2:12, 20. 3:6, 11, 17, 4:19). In the old covenant, doing good meant keeping the rules. In the new covenant, doing good is what we do when we have been apprehended by the goodness of God (1 Pet. 3:16), while doing right is living in right relationship with the Righteous One, who bore all our sins (1 Pet. 2:24).

Grace. The grace of God is the defining characteristic of the new covenant. The prophets of the Old Testament looked forward to the grace to come (1 Pet. 1:10), which has now been revealed through the gospel (1 Pet. 1:12). Peter proclaims a God of all grace (1 Pet. 5:10), who calls us so that we might be blessed (1 Pet. 3:9), and who freely gives grace to all who ask for it (1 Pet. 5:5). Because the manifold grace of God meets your every need

(1 Pet. 4:10), Peter prayed that God's grace would abound in your life (1 Pet. 1:2, 2 Pet. 1:2). God's grace abounds as we grow in our understanding of his Son and what he has done for us (2 Pet. 3:18). The true grace of God can be contrasted with the counterfeit and licentious grace preached by false teachers (1 Pet. 5:12, 2 Pet. 2:1–2).

Holy. In the old covenant, holiness was something to strive for and never achieve, but in the new covenant, believers have been sanctified by the Holy Spirit (1 Pet. 1:2). We are a holy people and a holy nation (1 Pet. 2:5, 9). Because believers are the holy offspring of a holy Father (1 Pet. 1:17), we can live holy and beautiful lives (1 Pet. 1:15–16, 2 Pet. 3:11). To act any other way would be contrary to your new nature.

Hope, A living. The gospel announces a resurrected and living Savior giving us a living hope (1 Pet. 1:3). If faith is the confidence believers have for today, hope is the confidence we have for tomorrow (1 Pet. 1:13, 3:15).

Judgment. In the new covenant, we are not judged for our sins, but by our response to the Savior. Those who are judged are those who don't obey the gospel of God (1 Pet. 4:17), are disobedient to the word (1 Pet. 2:8), and disbelieve (1 Pet. 2:7).

Knowledge. The old covenant the emphasis was on *doing*, but the new covenant emphasis is on *knowing* – knowing God and Jesus our Lord (2 Pet. 1:2) and knowing the way of righteousness (2 Pet. 2:21). Peter writes so that we might know that we have been redeemed with the blood of Christ (1 Pet. 1:18–19) and to remind us of truths that we already know (2 Pet. 1:12). Spiritual growth comes through the true knowledge of him who called us (2 Pet. 1:3). For this reason Peter encourages us to grow in the grace and knowledge of our Lord Jesus Christ (2 Pet. 3:18).

Love. Peter writes much about our love for Christ (1 Pet. 1:8) and our brothers and sisters (1 Pet. 1:22, 2:17, 5:14). We honor the Lord, who laid down his life for us, by loving and submitting to our husbands (1 Pet. 3:1), our wives (1 Pet. 3:7), our elders (1 Pet. 5:5a), our bosses (1 Pet. 2:18), and those in authority (1 Pet. 2:13). Peter describes a love that is other-focused and clothed with humility towards others (1 Pet. 5:5b).

New life. Peter contrasts the new life we have in Christ with the futile way of life we inherited from our ancestors (1 Pet. 1:18). When we didn't know any better, we lived for the desires of our flesh and without regard for the things of God (1 Pet. 1:14). But now, through the power and promises of God, we can participate in Christ's divine life (2 Pet. 1:4). Everything we need to enjoy this new life comes through knowing Christ (2 Pet. 1:3, 3:18).

Precious. In a world of mixed-up values, Peter highlights those things that are truly precious. We have been redeemed by the precious blood of Christ (1 Pet. 1:19), we stand on the precious promises of God (2 Pet. 1:4), and our God-given faith is more precious than gold (1 Pet. 1:7). In God's kingdom, Jesus is the precious cornerstone on which all else stands (1 Pet. 2:4, 6–7).

Redemption. In the old covenant, a sinner had to sacrifice a lamb that was without blemish, but in the new covenant, you have been redeemed by the superior sacrifice of the sinless Son of God (1 Pet. 2:22). You belong to God (1 Pet. 2:9). You can be sure that the One who paid such a high price for you (1 Pet. 1:18–19) will keep you safe and secure to the end.

Reminded. Forgetting what God has done renders us useless and unfruitful (2 Pet. 1:8). For this reason, we need to be reminded often of God's gracious provision (2 Pet. 1:12–13) and his forgiveness of all our sins (1 Pet. 3:18, 2 Pet. 1:9). We also need to be reminded to be ready and waiting for the Lord's return (2 Pet. 3:1–2).

Resurrection. The resurrection of Jesus is what makes the good news, *good news*. Peter was an eye-witness of the resurrection and refers to it several times (1 Pet. 1:3, 21, 3:21). Because Jesus was raised to new life, we have a living hope and an imperishable inheritance (1 Pet. 1:3–4, 23).

Righteousness. In the old covenant, righteousness, or the state of being right with God, was defined in terms of compliance with the law. But in the new covenant our right-standing is based on the righteousness of God (2 Pet. 1:1). The astonishing announcement of grace is that the Just justifies the unjust (1 Pet. 3:18). Because Jesus died for all our sin, we can live in right relationship with God (1 Pet. 2:24).

Salvation means deliverance from the doomed life we inherited from our forefathers (1 Pet. 1:10, 18). Peter highlights two aspects of salvation. When he speaks of the baptism that now saves us (1 Pet. 3:21), he is referring to the baptism into Christ done to every believer by the Holy Spirit. And when he speaks of the salvation to be revealed (1 Pet. 1:5), he is referring to the redemption of our bodies that will happen when Christ returns in glory. In either case, salvation means we have eternal life and an entrance into the eternal kingdom of our Lord (2 Pet. 1:11).

Savior. Peter refers to Jesus as our God and Savior (2 Pet. 1:1). The Risen Son, who is one with the Father, is well able to save you and provide everything you need to bring you into his eternal kingdom (2 Pet. 1:11).

Supply. The message of grace is that God supplies all you need. He supplies you with faith (2 Pet. 1:1), the strength to serve (1 Pet. 4:11), and everything else you need for life and godliness (2 Pet. 1:3). Truly he has abundantly provided you with an entrance into his kingdom (2 Pet. 1:11).

The will of God is one of Peter's favorite phrases (1 Pet. 2:15, 4:2, 6, 19, 5:2). It is not God's will for any to perish, but for all to come to repentance (2 Pet. 3:9). It is God's will for you to no longer walk in the old way of the flesh (1 Pet. 4:2), but to live in the spirit by trusting in his Son (1 Pet. 4:6). It is God's will for you to honor and pray for those in authority and bear up patiently under unjust suffering (1 Pet. 2:13–14, 20).

Word of God. God's word is powerful and creative (2 Pet. 3:5). You were born again through the Living Word of God, which is Jesus Christ (1 Pet. 1:23). Like newborn babies, we are to crave the pure milk of the word (1 Pet. 2:2), which means we grow in grace by learning more about Jesus (2 Pet. 3:18). Because the word of the Lord endures forever (1 Pet. 1:25), those who receive his life-giving word will endure forever.

1 Peter 1

1 Peter 1:1–2

[1] Peter, an apostle of Jesus Christ, to those who reside as aliens, scattered throughout Pontus, Galatia, Cappadocia, Asia, and Bithynia, who are chosen. [2] according to the foreknowledge of God the Father, by the sanctifying work of the Spirit, to obey Jesus Christ and be sprinkled with his blood: May grace and peace be yours in the fullest measure.

1:1 **Peter** was one of the first disciples to be called and he became one of the Lord's closest friends (Mark 1:16). His given name was Simon (2 Pet. 1:1), but the Lord called him Peter (John 1:42). He witnessed the Lord's transfiguration (2 Pet. 1:17–18) and crucifixion (1 Pet. 5:1), and he was the first apostle to see the Risen Lord (Luke 24:34, 1 Cor. 15:5).

Apostle means delegate or ambassador, or someone who has been sent. An apostle is someone who has been sent out as a messenger for God. In a sense, we are all called to be God's messengers or ambassadors (2 Cor. 5:20). But in the church, some are uniquely gifted and called to be apostles (1 Cor. 12:28–29).

Aliens. The original word (*parepidemos*) means foreign resident.

Scattered. The original word (*diaspora*) means dispersed and usually describes Jews living in Gentile nations. Peter was writing to Christian Jews who had fled Judea on account of the persecution that came against the early church (Acts 8:1, 11:19). Those who were scattered settled in foreign countries and preached the gospel (Acts 8:4). Churches were planted and Gentiles were welcomed into the family of God. Although Peter wrote to encourage scattered individuals, his letter was circulated among churches led by elders (see 1 Pet. 5:1).

Pontus, Galatia, Cappadocia, Asia, and Bithynia were five Roman provinces in Asia Minor (modern-day Turkey). Peter sent a letter to the churches in these provinces and the letter was delivered by his good friend Silvanus (1 Pet. 5:12). Later, he sent a second letter (2 Pet. 3:1).

Chosen. You have been chosen by God (Eph. 1:4, 2 Th. 2:13, 2 Tim. 2:10). In the New Testament believers are referred to as the elect or chosen of God (Rom. 8:33, Col. 3:12, Tit. 1:1). "Many are called, but few are chosen," said Jesus (Matt. 22:14). Those who respond to the call of God are called the elect or the chosen. "For you are a chosen generation" (1 Pet. 2:9). In a manner of speaking, the chosen choose themselves by responding to the call of God. But since the Lord initiates the call, it's accurate to say we are God's chosen.

1:2 **Foreknowledge**. The God who sees the end from the beginning knew who would respond to the gospel (Rom. 8:29, Eph. 1:4–5). Before time began he wrote their names in the Book of Life (Rev. 17:8).

God the Father; see next verse.

The sanctifying work of the Spirit. You were chosen by God (see previous verse) and set apart by the Holy Spirit. You are not sanctified on account of anything you have done. You were sanctified through the sacrifice of Jesus (Heb. 10:14). You are part of a holy priesthood (1 Pet. 2:5).

To obey Jesus Christ is to heed his call to repent and believe the gospel (Mark 1:15). In contrast, unbelievers are those who do not obey the gospel of God (1 Pet. 4:17).

Sprinkled with his blood. Just as Moses ratified the old covenant by sprinkling the blood of sacrifices on the Israelites (Ex. 24:8), the new covenant was ratified with the better blood of the Lamb (Heb. 9:22, 12:24).

Grace and peace; see 2 Pet. 1:2.

The fullest measure. May God's grace be yours in increasing abundance. Grace is not merely for your salvation; grace is for partaking in the divine life that Christ offers to all of us. Grace saves us, keeps us, protects us, and blesses us (1 Pet. 5:10). We grow in grace by growing in the knowledge of our Lord and Savior Jesus Christ (2 Pet 3:18).

---

1 Peter 1:3–5

3 Blessed be the God and Father of our Lord Jesus Christ, who
according to his great mercy has caused us to be born again to a living hope through the resurrection of Jesus Christ from the dead, 4 to
obtain an inheritance which is imperishable and undefiled and will
not fade away, reserved in heaven for you, 5 who are protected by
the power of God through faith for a salvation ready to be revealed
in the last time.

1:3 **God and Father**. God is the Father of Jesus (John 8:54), but he is also the Father of all who have been born again (1 Pet. 1:17).

Great mercy. Just as God has great grace (Jas. 4:6), he has great mercy (Luke 1:58). God is both rich in grace (Eph. 1:7, 2:7), and mercy (Eph. 2:4). His great mercy testifies to his great love for us (Eph. 2:4).

Born again. The original word (*anagennao*) means to beget. You are begotten by God and his imperishable seed abides in you (1 Pet. 1:23, 1 John 3:9).

In this letter Peter describes two wonderful things that have happened to the believer; (1) you have been redeemed (1 Pet. 1:18), and (2) you have been born again. Because you were redeemed, you could be born again, and because you were born again, everything has changed. The moment you put your faith in the Son of God, you crossed over from death to new life (John 5:24). You left Adam's doomed family and were adopted into the family of God (Rom. 8:15). Because your rebirth was an act of God, you cannot undo what the Lord has done. Because you have been born of imperishable seed, you are eternally saved and eternally secure.

A living hope is a hope in a risen Lord who gives life and hope to the dead. Jesus who died but now lives is our living hope.

This world will crush your hopes and dreams, but your heavenly Father does not want you to become weary and hopeless. You have a great need for hope; you have a great God who meets your need (Rom. 15:13).

The resurrection is what makes the good news *good news* for it proves that Jesus is the Holy and Righteous Savior. If Jesus had been a fraud, God would not have raised him. But Jesus rose and ascended to heaven and now sits at the right hand of God (Mark 16:19). The Author of Life conquered the grave and now holds the keys of death and Hades (Rev. 1:18). For those of us clothed with mortal bodies, this is a source of great comfort and hope.

1:4 **An inheritance** that is imperishable refers to eternal life. In one sense, eternal life is something we enjoy now through our union with Christ (John 17:3). But an *unfading* and *imperishable* inheritance that is reserved in heaven refers to the glorious resurrection body we will receive when Christ returns.

Reserved in heaven. Your resurrection life is kept safe for you in heaven, where sin and disease cannot touch it. Aware that his earthly life would soon be taken from him (2 Pet. 1:14), Peter was looking forward to a resurrection body that no one can harm.

1:5 **Protected**. The original word (*phroureo*) means garrisoned or guarded. The Lord is your Guardian and Keeper who protects you with his mighty power (1 Pet. 2:25). Nothing in life or death can separate you from his love (Rom. 8:38–39).

Power of God. You are not protected because you believe right or pray right. You are protected because God is powerful. Consider Peter. On his worst night his courage failed him, but he was not lost because Jesus was praying for him (Luke 22:32).

It may seem strange to say that Christians who were being persecuted and sometimes martyred for their faith were powerfully protected by the power of God, but Peter is talking about the salvation of their souls, not their bodies (1 Pet. 1:9). Your body may age and decay, but you – the real, inner you – will not be lost. And when Jesus is revealed from heaven, you will be clothed with a resurrection body that will never fade away or die.

Faith. All of God's blessings, including his protection, come to us freely by grace and are received by faith. You are not protected because you diligently pray prayers or psalms of protection. Nor are you protected because you confess and keep short accounts with the Lord. You are protected by the mighty power of God. Your part is to trust him and rest in his grace, knowing that he who watches over you will neither slumber nor sleep (Ps. 121:4).

Salvation to be revealed. In Christ, we are born again, and 100 percent saved. Yet we are still looking forward to the redemption of our bodies (Rom. 8:23). Our present bodies age and decay, but one day we will be clothed in glory. When Jesus returns, we will be changed and that which is mortal shall be clothed in immortality. The perishable will put on the imperishable and death will be swallowed up in victory (1 Cor. 15:53–54).

Revealed. The original word (*apokalupto*) means uncover and disclose. Who we are has not been fully disclosed. But when Jesus returns, the real, glorious, imperishable you will be revealed (Col. 3:4, 1 Pet. 5:1).

In the last time. The last days; see 1 Pet. 1:20.

---

1 Peter 1:6–7

6 In this you greatly rejoice, even though now for a little while, if
necessary, you have been distressed by various trials, 7 so that the
proof of your faith, being more precious than gold which is perishable, even though tested by fire, may be found to result in praise and glory and honor at the revelation of Jesus Christ;

1:6 **Greatly rejoice**. God's promise to watch over us is a source of great joy and comfort as we face life's trials.

For the believer there is a joy that comes from knowing the shadowless love and acceptance of the Father (see 1 Pet. 1:8). Yet there is also another kind of joy that we can experience in the midst of our trials (Jas. 1:2). The latter joy comes from knowing that what the enemy intends for evil, our Redeemer will repurpose for good (Rom. 8:28).

A little while; see 1 Pet. 5:10.

Various trials. Trials and tribulations are a normal part of the Christian life (2 Tim. 3:12), but the recipients of Peter's letter were experiencing harsh and unjust suffering on account of their faith (1 Pet. 2:19–20). They were being slandered as evildoers (1 Pet. 2:12, 3:16) and they were experiencing a fiery ordeal (1 Pet. 4:12). What form that persecution took we can only guess. It could be that they were being plundered or losing their homes (Heb. 10:34, Rev. 2:9). However, a *fiery* ordeal suggests something more serious (see 1 Pet. 4:17).

1:7 **Proof**. The original word (*dokimion*) means proving in the way an assayer tests and approves gold.

The proof of your faith. Just as some materials get stronger when compressed, your God-given faith reveals its supernatural qualities when you go through trials.

The trials of life are not to see whether we are made of the right stuff or whether we can whip up enough faith, for we can't manufacture faith at all. Faith is something to receive (2 Pet. 1:1). Faith that endures is a gift from God and we get it from hearing the good news of Jesus (Eph. 2:8).

More precious than gold. Just as gold is purified through fire, the precious quality of our God-given faith is revealed when we go through fiery trials.

Praise and glory and honor. No matter what life dishes out, the children of God will stand blameless and confident before the Lord on the day that he is revealed (1 Cor. 1:8, 1 John 4:17). All this is to the glory of the Shepherd who watches over us and sustains us to the end (1 Pet. 2:25).

The revelation of Jesus Christ refers to the final coming when the Son of Man is revealed from heaven (Luke 17:30, 2 Th. 1:7). Peter also refers to this event as the day of the Lord (2 Pet. 3:10), the day of God (2 Pet. 3:12), the day of visitation (1 Pet. 2:12), the day of judgment (2 Pet. 2:9, 3:7), and the day of eternity (2 Pet. 3:18).

1 Peter 1:8–9

[8] and though you have not seen him, you love him, and though you do not see him now, but believe in him, you greatly rejoice with joy inexpressible and full of glory, [9] obtaining as the outcome of your faith the salvation of your souls.

1:8 **You have not seen him**. Peter had seen Jesus and witnessed his earthly ministry (1 Pet. 5:1), but we have not seen him.

You love him... believe in him. When you know how good God is and how deeply he loves you, he is easy to trust (1 John 2:5).

You do not see him now. We cannot see Jesus in his physical form until the day he is revealed (2 Cor. 5:16). But we can know him through the eyes and ears of faith.

Joy inexpressible. Trusting the Risen Lord brings us great joy. Knowing that he is with us through thick and thin and that he will complete the good work he has begun in our lives fills our hearts with gladness.

1:9 **The outcome of your faith** is salvation from death. It is eternal life.

There are different types of faith. The religious Jews had faith in God but theirs was not a saving faith because it was unaccompanied by the work of believing in the Savior he sent (Jas. 2:14). But we who have obeyed Jesus Christ (1 Pet. 1:2) and believed in him (1 Pet. 2:6) have the same faith as the apostles (2 Pet. 1:1) – a faith that leads to salvation (2 Tim. 3:15). "For by grace you have been saved through faith" (Eph. 2:8).

Your faith comes from the Lord. It is not something you manufacture, but something you receive (2 Pet. 1:1). Faith comes from hearing about the love of God revealed in Jesus (Rom. 10:17).

The salvation of your souls will be fully realized when the Lord returns, and we are clothed in glory (1 Pet. 1:5).

Some speak of salvation as though it was an ongoing process. That is not what Peter is talking about here. If you are in

Christ, you are a new creation, fully saved and fully sanctified. Your soul has been purified by truth (1 Pet. 1:22). Yet our physical bodies remain subject to decay. In our bodies we engage with sin and experience its deathly effects (Rom. 6:6, 12). But when Jesus Christ is revealed from heaven, we will be clothed with resurrection bodies that cannot be touched by sin (1 Cor. 15:52, Php. 3:21).

---

1 Peter 1:10–12

[10] As to this salvation, the prophets who prophesied of the grace that
would come to you made careful searches and inquiries, [11] seeking
to know what person or time the Spirit of Christ within them was
indicating as he predicted the sufferings of Christ and the glories to
follow. [12] It was revealed to them that they were not serving themselves, but you, in these things which now have been announced to
you through those who preached the gospel to you by the Holy Spirit
sent from heaven—things into which angels long to look.

1:10 **Salvation**. The original word for salvation means deliverance or rescue. In context, salvation means deliverance from death and the futile or doomed life we inherited from our forefathers (1 Pet. 1:18).

The grace that would come through Jesus Christ (John 1:17). Although the Old Testament prophets lived under the law covenant, they knew through the Holy Spirit that a better covenant of grace was coming. The prophets who prophesied of the grace to come included Isaiah (Is. 54:10), Jeremiah (Jer. 31:31–34), and Ezekiel (Eze. 37:26–27).

Careful searches. Having received revelation from the Holy Spirit, the Old Testament prophets were understandably curious about the grace to come. Who? What? When? How? What they longed for, we have received.

1:11 **What person or time**. The Old Testament prophets knew by the Holy Spirit that a Savior was coming to redeem humanity, but who and when? They sensed the plan, but they did not know the details. Only now, in the fullness of time, has God revealed his hand. The details of his rescue plan are known to us as the gospel (see next verse).

The Spirit of Christ within them. Although the Holy Spirit had not been poured out prior to the Day of Pentecost (John 7:39), he revealed the coming Messiah to the Old Testament prophets.

The sufferings... the glories. The Old Testament prophets foretold the crucifixion of Christ (e.g., Is. 53:6–9) and his glorious ascension and return (e.g., Ps. 68:18, Zech. 9:14).

1:12 **It was revealed** to the Old Testament prophets by the Holy Spirit that a Savior was coming, and they recorded these revelations for our benefit. Now, through the gospel preachers of the new covenant, the Holy Spirit has announced and continues to announce the good news that the Savior has come.

Announced. The gospel is an announcement of the glad tidings of a happy God that brings great joy to all (Luke 2:10). Manmade religion tells you what to do; the gospel announces what has been done. Reconciliation, acceptance, and forgiveness are not rewards to earn, but gifts to receive on account of what Christ has done.

Those who preached. The gospel has to be preached to be heard (Rom. 10:14). Preachers like Paul and Silas had gone to Asia and Galatia to preach the good news to the recipients of this letter (see 1 Pet. 5:12).

The gospel is the good news that God so loved the world that he gave us his Son (John 3:16). See also the entry for 1 Peter 4:17.

The Holy Spirit or the Spirit of Christ (1 Pet. 1:11) or the Spirit of glory (1 Pet. 4:14). Peter heard the Lord promise that the Father would send the Holy Spirit (John 14:26), and Peter was present on the Day of Pentecost when the Holy Spirit came (Acts 2:1–4).

Angels. The prophets looked forward and the angels looked down to see the marvelous rescue plan that God had prepared for us.

1 Peter 1:13–16

[13] Therefore, prepare your minds for action, keep sober in spirit, fix your hope completely on the grace to be brought to you at the revelation of Jesus Christ. [14] As obedient children, do not be conformed to the former lusts which were yours in your ignorance, [15] but like the Holy One who called you, be holy yourselves also in all your behavior; [16] because it is written, "You shall be holy, for I am holy."

1:13 **Prepare your minds for action**. Don't be passive, but put your faith to work. Fortify your mind with the promises of God so that you may walk in newness of life and participate in his divine nature (2 Pet. 1:4).

Keep sober in spirit. Be clearheaded and live with your eyes open. Don't be so preoccupied with your appetites that you let the opportunity for real life pass you by. Life is short (Jas. 1:11). Live with eternity in mind.

Fix your hope on the risen Lord who gives life to the dead (1 Pet. 1:3).

Hope. The gospel points you to the God of hope and leaves you abounding in supernatural hope.

Hope is a rope that links us to truth and there is no greater Truth to which you can affix your "hope-rope" than God himself. At one time we were, "without hope and without God," but "on him we have set our hope" (Eph. 2:12, 2 Cor. 1:9–10). The God of hope will never let you down.

Grace; see 1 Pet. 5:5.

The revelation of Jesus Christ. The glorious return of the Lord Jesus; see 1 Pet. 1:7.

1:14 **Obedient children**. Believers are known as the children of God (1 John 3:1). We obey our Father because we know how good he is and how much he loves us.

In the old covenant, obedience was defined as compliance to a set of laws. But in the new covenant obedience is the fruit of trusting Jesus. Because we have come to realize that God is good, we have confidence in his Son (1 John 3:23).

The former lusts are the desires of your old and futile way of life when you walked after the flesh, were captive to your appetites, and gave no thought to the things of God.

Ignorance. When you were an unbeliever and didn't know there was a better way to live.

1:15 **The Holy One** is the Lord God. Although the Holy One is usually a reference to the Son of God (e.g., Mark 1:24, John 6:69, Acts 2:27), the context here suggests God the Father. It is "the God of all grace who called you to his eternal glory in Christ" (1 Pet. 5:10). Jesus referred to God as his Holy Father (John 17:11).

Who called you. God's call to turn to him and be saved goes out to the ends of the earth (Is. 45:22). He calls all of us, Jew and Gentile alike, to come out of darkness and enter into his wonderful light (1 Cor. 1:24, 1 Pet. 2:9). Not everyone responds to his call, but those who do are known as the called of Jesus Christ (Rom. 1:6).

Be holy because you are a holy priesthood and a holy nation (1 Pet. 2:5, 9). You are the holy offspring of your Holy Father. So *be* holy because you *are* holy. To act any other way is contrary to your new nature.

Some say holy behavior is an unobtainable goal. It's something to strive for knowing that you will never hit the mark while you are in your earthly body. Yet Christ's perfections more than compensate for our imperfections, and Christ the Holy One lives in you. Learn to see your body as a holy and living sacrifice, totally acceptable to God (Rom. 12:1).

In all your behavior. Behavior follows identity. When you know who you are – a holy child of the Holy Father – you will know how to act. We are not made holy because we act holy, but we will act holy when we realize that we are holy people. The New Testament is peppered with exhortations to be holy (Eph. 1:4, 1 Th. 4:7, Heb. 12:14, 1 Pet. 1:15, 2 Pet. 3:11, Rev. 22:11). We are called to be holy because in Christ we are holy.

1:16 **Written**. The quote comes from Leviticus 11:45: "For I am the Lord who brought you up from the land of Egypt to be your God; thus you shall be holy, for I am holy." This passage is significant for it is the first time in the Bible that God is described as holy.

Under the old covenant, the command to be holy was bad news because no one can be as holy as God. But in the new covenant, the exhortation to be holy is a thrilling invitation to the holy and beautiful life that is ours in Christ. Because you are begotten by a holy Father, you are holy and can be holy in all you do (1 Cor. 1:2, Heb. 10:10). Holiness is not something to work for but a gift to receive and enjoy.

I am holy. God is the definition of holiness.

God is holy and holy is his name (Luke 1:49). To say God is holy is to refer to the wholeness, fullness, beauty, and abundant life that overflows within the Godhead. God lacks nothing. In contrast with sinful humanity, he is unbroken, undamaged, unfallen, completely complete and entire within himself. He is the indivisible One, wholly self-sufficient, and the picture of perfection.

---

1 Peter 1:17–19

[17] If you address as Father the One who impartially judges according
to each one's work, conduct yourselves in fear during the time of
your stay on earth; [18] knowing that you were not redeemed with perishable things like silver or gold from your futile way of life inherited
from your forefathers, [19] but with precious blood, as of a lamb unblemished and spotless, the blood of Christ.

1:17 **Father**. What makes the new covenant *new* is that we recognize God as our heavenly Father and ourselves as his dearly-loved children.

An old covenant mindset causes you to view God as a bookkeeper recording your sins or a judge condemning your failures. But Jesus revealed a God who loves you like a Father (John 16:27). In the old covenant, no one dared to address the

Almighty in familiar terms. But after Jesus, every New Testament writer did.

Each one's work. We are judged by what we have done with Jesus.

This verse is a favorite of those who preach works. "One day God will judge the good works you have done in this life." But if we could stand before God on the basis of our works, we would have no need for grace. Or Jesus. Our righteous works are like filthy rags (Is. 64:6).

On several occasions Peter heard the Lord talk about being judged or repaid for what we have done (Matt. 16:27, John 5:29). Peter came to understand that the only work that counts with God is the work of believing in the One he has sent. Believing in the Lord Jesus Christ is the action that reveals our faith (John 6:29).

Conduct yourselves in fear means live in reverence and awe of God.

Although the original word for fear (*phobos*) literally means fear, Peter's use of this word in other contexts suggests reverence or deference (e.g., 1 Pet. 3:2). In the new covenant, to fear the Lord is to worship and revere him (see 1 Pet. 2:17). Peter is saying, "If you know God as your heavenly Father, let your conduct on earth be your spiritual act of worship."

Why worship the Lord? In the opening chapter of his letter Peter gives us several reasons. We worship the Lord because he redeemed us from bondage with the precious blood of Christ (1 Pet. 1:18–19); he has given us rebirth through imperishable seed into new life (1 Pet. 1:23); he has sanctified us by his Spirit (1 Pet. 1:2); he is reserving for us an eternal inheritance (1 Pet. 1:4), and he protects us with his mighty power (1 Pet. 1:5).

1:18 **Redeemed**. To be redeemed is to be ransomed. You were a slave of sin, but a free Man from heaven purchased you and now you are free (Gal. 5:1).

Throughout history many pseudo-saviors have come promising freedom, but every one of them was a slave to sin. They couldn't save anyone (Ps. 49:7–8). We needed a free man to redeem us and Jesus is the free Man who gave his life as a ransom for all (1 Tim. 2:6).

Perishable things. You weren't ransomed with something as common as silver or gold but with the precious blood of Christ.

Your futile way of life. The original word for futile (*mataios*) means empty or useless. Such was the life we had when we lived for our appetites and without regard for the things of God (1 Pet. 1:14).

Forefathers. Your family tree is riddled with sinners from Adam all the way down to your ancestors. We act like sinners because that is how the world teaches us to act.

1:19 **Precious blood**. You were ransomed with the most valuable substance in the universe – the precious blood of God's only Son.

As of a lamb. Jesus is the Lamb of God who took away the sin of the world (John 1:29).

Unblemished and spotless. In the old covenant, a sinner had to sacrifice a lamb that was without blemish (Ex. 12:5). But in the new covenant, we have been eternally redeemed by the superior sacrifice of the sinless Son of God (1 Pet. 2:22).

---

1 Peter 1:20–23

[20] For he was foreknown before the foundation of the world, but has
appeared in these last times for the sake of you [21] who through him
are believers in God, who raised him from the dead and gave him
glory, so that your faith and hope are in God. [22] Since you have in
obedience to the truth purified your souls for a sincere love of the
brethren, fervently love one another from the heart, [23] for you have
been born again not of seed which is perishable but imperishable,
that is, through the living and enduring word of God.

1:20 **Foreknown**. God knew in advance that he would send his Son to redeem us (Rom. 8:29). Before Adam sinned and condemned humanity to death, God had a plan to rescue us.

These last times are the last days (2 Pet. 3:3). Some say the last days are the present generation, but last days or last times began 2000 years ago when Jesus began his earthly ministry (Heb. 1:2).

1:21 **Through him**. It is through the Son that we came to know and trust the Father (John 14:6).

Believers in God. Many religious people consider themselves believers in God, but unless they come to the Father through the Son their faith is dead and useless. It is not a saving faith (Jas. 2:14, 17).

God, who raised him. Although the religious Jews believed in God, they did not believe that he raised Jesus from the dead. They did not share the faith of those who were witnesses of the resurrection (2 Pet. 1:1).

Glory. The original noun (*doxa*) means majesty, magnificence, splendor, preeminence, and exalted.

Faith and hope. Our faith and hope are not in ourselves or our works; our faith and hope are in the Lord and his finished work.

1:22 **Obedience to the truth**. You obeyed Christ's call to believe the gospel (Mark 1:15). You obeyed God's command to believe in the Name of his Son (1 John 3:23).

Purified your souls. Our souls were purified when we heeded the truth of the gospel and were born again (1 Cor. 6:11, 1 John 1:7, 9).

The preacher of works misquotes this verse: "You need to purify your souls through prayer and discipline." But Peter says our souls *were* purified when we obeyed the truth and came to Jesus. Your soul is not filthy. When you were born again you were given a new heart and a new mind with new desires to please the Lord (Eze. 11:19, 36:26, 1 Cor. 2:16).

Fervently means with intent; see 1 Pet. 4:8.

Love one another. We don't purify our souls by loving others. Rather, we are able to love others because God first loved us (1 John 4:19). Love for our Christian brothers and sisters is a sign that someone is growing in the love and grace of God (2 Pet. 1:7, 1 John 3:14).

One another. Although we are called to share God's love with all people, the exhortation to love intentionally applies to "the brethren," meaning the household of God or fellow believers.

1:23 **Born again**; see 1 Pet. 1:3.

Seed. The imperishable seed is the living and enduring word of God (Luke 8:11). It is the spiritual DNA of Jesus himself (1 John 3:9). Jesus is the Word of life (1 John 1:1) who imparts life like a seed.

Imperishable. Because you have been born of imperishable seed, you are eternally saved and secure. No one can undo what the Lord has done and no one can snatch you from your Father's hand (John 10:29).

The word of God is most clearly revealed in his Son. Jesus is the Word made flesh and the Living Word of God (John 1:14, Rev. 19:13).

The word of God refers to the way God makes himself and his will known (1 Sam. 3:21). God's word is powerful, creative and sustains all things (2 Pet. 3:5). His word is the means by which the universe came into existence (Gen. 1:3, John 1:1), and his word gives life to the dead (Eze. 37:4). His word is a lamp that guides us in the path of life (Ps. 119:105), and his word always comes to pass (Is. 55:11).

Some people equate the word of God with the Bible. Although the Bible reveals the word of God, it would be incorrect to say you have been born again of the Bible. The imperishable seed that gives you new life is not the written word but the Living Word who dwells in you.

---

1 Peter 1:24–25

24 For, "All flesh is like grass, and all its glory like the flower of grass.
The grass withers, and the flower falls off, 25 but the word of the lord
endures forever." And this is the word which was preached to you.

1:24 **All flesh** withers and dies like grass. Life is a vapor that appears for a time then vanishes away (Jas. 4:14). In contrast, those who have been born again through the life-giving word of God, endure forever. This prophecy comes from Isaiah 40:6–8.

1:25 **The word of the Lord** created the heavens and the earth (2 Pet. 3:5). The creative word of the Lord fills you with new and lasting life.

Endures forever. In scripture, two things endure forever; the word of the Lord and the love of God (1 Cor. 13:7). When you know the love of God and allow the word of the Lord to take root in your heart, you will endure forever.

Preached. The creative life-giving word of God that was preached to you is the good news of Jesus Christ. Jesus is the Word of God made flesh who sustains all things and through whom all things were made (Col. 1:16, Heb. 1:3).

---

1 Peter 2

1 Peter 2:1–3

[1] Therefore, putting aside all malice and all deceit and hypocrisy and
envy and all slander, [2] like newborn babies, long for the pure milk of
the word, so that by it you may grow in respect to salvation, [3] if you
have tasted the kindness of the Lord.

2:1 **Therefore**. Because you have been born again of imperishable seed (1 Pet. 1:23), you can partake in the divine nature of Christ (2 Pet. 1:4).

Putting aside. Lay aside the old life and put on the new self. Many believers are trying to reform their old selves. They think that if they tried a little harder, they could make themselves good and holy. Peter demolishes that dead-end thinking. "You have been born again (1 Pet. 1:3, 23). You are a royal priesthood and a holy nation (1 Pet. 2:9)."

If Peter was an old covenant law preacher he would say, "Thou shalt not be malicious, deceitful, or hypocritical lest the hand of the Lord smite thee for thy disobedience." But Peter is a new covenant grace preacher who reminds us who we are (chosen, born again, holy, royal) and then shows us how to experience the new life that is already ours in Christ.

Malice, deceit, hypocrisy. Peter's list of fleshly deeds is similar to Paul's lists (Gal. 5:19–21, Eph. 4:31, Col. 3:8). All these things proceed from a selfish heart and corrupt us (Mark 7:20–23).

2:2 **Newborn babies** are known for their hunger and rapid growth. If we want to grow, we need to feed on the Bread of Life (John 6:51) and consume the pure milk of the Living Word.

Long for. The operative verb in this passage indicates we are to crave or earnestly desire the word. This does not mean we need to study the Bible for hours every day. It means we grow by feeding on Jesus the Living Word (see also 2 Pet. 3:18).

The pure milk of the word is the Living Word of God. It is the Lord himself (1 Pet. 1:23).

May grow. Growth is a natural process that can be hindered by malnutrition and poor diet (e.g., the cares of the world that choke the word (Matt. 13:22)).

Salvation. Growing in respect to salvation means growing into who you are in Christ. You are a child of God, so act like it. You are holy, so be holy (1 Pet. 1:15). Be who you truly are. This is Peter's version of "work out your salvation with fear and trembling" (Php. 2:12).

2:3 **If you have tasted** or "if you are a believer." Peter is speaking to "you who believe" (1 Pet. 2:7).

Two kinds of people tasted the kindness of the Lord. There are those who have heard the gospel, but they have not allowed it to take root in their heart and grow (Jas. 1:21). They've had a taste but spat it out.

Then there are those who have received the word with thanksgiving and faith and have been born again (1 Pet. 1:23). Peter is talking to the second group here. He is saying, "If you have tasted that the Lord is good, then taste some more. Crave the pure milk of his word and grow. Feast on his goodness and be satisfied."

Tasted. Peter is riffing on Psalm 34:8: "O taste and see that the Lord is good." The Hebrew word for good in this psalm is an expansive word that means beautiful, best, better, bountiful, cheerful, at ease, favour, fine, glad, joyful, kindly, loving, merry, pleasure, precious, prosperity, ready, sweet, wealth, welfare. The Lord is the very definition of good.

Some Bibles translate Peter's words as "if you have tasted that the Lord is *gracious*." The kindness or graciousness of God was demonstrated on the cross (Tit. 3:4), and it is his kindness that leads us to repentance (Rom. 2:4). God reveals his grace and kindness to us today, tomorrow and forever more (1 Cor. 2:9, Eph. 2:7).

A choice stone. The original word for choice (*eklektos*) is the same word which is sometimes translated as chosen (e.g., Luke 23:35). Jesus is both the choice stone and the Chosen of God.

Cornerstone. The cornerstone is the first stone laid in a new structure. As such, it sets a mark for the rest of the building. Jesus is the cornerstone on which God's house is being built (Eph. 2:20).

He who believes in him. The chief takeaway of the new covenant is to believe in the Lord Jesus Christ (John 3:16).

Will not be disappointed. You will never regret putting your faith in the Lord.

In his original prophecy, Isaiah said, "He who believes in it (the costly cornerstone) will not be disturbed" or panicked or be in haste. Peter interprets this as "not be disappointed" or disgraced or put to shame. (Paul draws a similar conclusion in Romans 9:33.) Put your faith in imperfect people and you will be disappointed, but the Lord will never let you down. His love never fails (1 Cor. 13:8).

2:7 **Precious value**. Unlike those who reject Jesus, believers honor Jesus as the cornerstone of God's habitation, and the foundation of his redemptive purposes.

The original word for precious value (*time*) is the same word that is translated elsewhere as honor (1 Pet. 1:7, 3:7, 2 Pet. 1:17). Believers honor Jesus Christ as the Son sent to save us, the high priest who represents us, and the Lord whose Name is above all.

The stone which the builders rejected. Peter starts with a prophecy (see previous verse), then segues into a psalm (Ps. 118:22). This psalm must have been one of his favorites for he included it in his sermon on the Day of Pentecost (Acts 4:11). Perhaps he was inspired by the Lord who also quoted this psalm (see Matt. 21:42).

The builders. The Jews were so proud of the temple they had built that they bragged to Jesus about its magnificent stones (Mark 13:1). In their minds, they had created something that would impress God himself. Yet when the Son of God and the

Living Stone showed up, they didn't want to know him. Those who are trying to impress the Lord with their works and sacrifices are dishonoring the Lord and his sacrifice.

2:8 **A stone of stumbling**. Jesus is the cornerstone (Ps. 118:22, Is. 28:16, Zech. 10:4, Eph. 2:20), the top stone (Zech. 4:7), and the living stone (1 Pet. 2:4) who is in the path of every person. Either we will fall on the stone and be broken in repentance (Matt. 21:44), or we will stumble over the stone offended. The unbelieving Jews were in the second group.

A rock of offense. Those who have invested their lives in works of righteousness are offended by the message of grace. They do not care to hear that their good works count for nothing in the economy of grace.

They stumble. By rejecting God's Son, the Jews stumbled or fell from their privileged position as God's chosen people (Rom. 9:31–32).

Disobedient to the word. The original word for disobedient (*apeitheo*) means to disbelieve. Those who are disobedient, such as the religious Jews who rejected the cornerstone, disobey Christ's call to repent and believe the gospel (Mark 1:15).

This doom they were also appointed. Those who trust in themselves and their works will fall, and this was foreseen by the prophets (e.g., Is. 8:14–15).

---

1 Peter 2:9–10

9 But you are a chosen race, a royal priesthood, a holy nation, a people for God's own possession, so that you may proclaim the excellencies of him who has called you out of darkness into his marvelous light; 10 for you once were not a people, but now you are the people of God; you had not received mercy, but now you have received mercy.

2:9 **But you**. Believers (1 Pet. 1:8). Those who see Jesus as the precious cornerstone (1 Pet. 2:6–7).

A chosen race. Believers are God's tribe, his kin and household. Once upon a time, we were part of Adam's family. But then we were chosen and adopted into the family of God (Rom. 8:15).

A royal priesthood. Like Melchizedek, who was a king and a priest (Heb. 7:1), Christians are king-priests or priest-kings (Rev. 1:6, 5:10).

If we are to rule and reign in the Name of the Servant-king, we need to understand our dual vocation as kings and priests. If you get the priestly part but not the kingly part, you'll be servant-minded instead of servant-hearted. And if you get the kingly aspect but not the priestly part, you'll be a tyrant. As kingly-priests we minister with power and authority. As priestly kings we rule as servant-hearted ministers.

A holy nation. We are a holy priesthood, a holy house, and a holy nation. You are not primarily an American, Australian, or Argentinian. You are a Christian, a citizen of a heavenly kingdom and a holy nation belonging to God.

This wonderful promise was originally given to the nation of Israel (Ex. 19:5–6), but the Jews broke the covenant and cut themselves off from God through unbelief. Now the blessings promised to the children of Abraham are for all who share Abraham's faith (Gal. 3:9).

God's own possession. You have been bought with a price (1 Cor. 6:20, 7:23, Tit. 2:14). Since you belong to God, your welfare is his concern. You can be sure that the One who paid such a high price for you can be trusted to keep you safe and secure to the end (1 Cor. 1:8–9).

In the old covenant, the Israelites were told they would be a treasured possession if they kept the law (Ex. 19:5–6). But the new covenant reveals that you are a treasured possession because God loves and treasures you. You are the pearl of great price. Jesus happily gave everything he had to purchase you.

So that you may proclaim the excellencies of him who has called you. To proclaim (*exaggello*) is to publish or show forth. The original word is related to the word for messenger (*aggellos*). As believers, we have been called to proclaim the message of God's salvation. That doesn't mean we will all be preachers behind a pulpit, but we are all called to shine with the gifts that God has given us (1 Pet. 4:10).

The excellencies or praises (*arete*) of God refer to his manly attributes in rescuing us from the kingdom of darkness. Although God's nature has feminine and nurturing characteristics (e.g., Is. 49:15, 66:13, Luke 13:34), his mighty deliverance is portrayed here in masculine terms.

Who has called you. God did not negotiate with the powers of darkness to secure your release. Nor did he engage in some kind of prisoner exchange. When God called you, you came because the word of the king has power (Ecc. 8:4).

Out of darkness. Darkness is a metaphor for evil and sin and anything untouched by the God-who-is-light. Any place the good news of Jesus is not heard or received remains in darkness.

His marvelous light. The light of God's love is revealed in Jesus Christ, the light of life and the light of the world (John 8:12).

2:10 **Not a people**. Once upon a time, we were nobodies.

The people of God. But now we are somebodies, the dearly-loved children of God (1 John 3:1).

In context, Peter is speaking to believers in churches across five Roman provinces (1 Pet. 1:1). These churches probably contained mixed audiences of Jewish and Gentile believers.

Received mercy. Every believer has received God's grace and mercy.

Mercy is one facet of God's grace (Heb. 4:16). Mercy is God's compassion for those in need. Just as we are saved by grace (Eph. 2:5), we are saved by mercy (Tit. 3:5). And just as we are forgiven by grace (Eph. 1:7), we are forgiven by mercy (Heb. 8:12). Just as we receive grace (Rom. 5:17), we receive mercy (2 Cor. 4:1).

Some people beg God for mercy as though God were harsh and aloof, but the gospel declares God's mercy has been freely given and all we need to do is receive it. The mercy we need is found at the throne of grace (Heb. 4:16).

1 Peter 2:11–12

[11] Beloved, I urge you as aliens and strangers to abstain from fleshly lusts which wage war against the soul. [12] Keep your behavior excellent among the Gentiles, so that in the thing in which they slander you as evildoers, they may because of your good deeds, as they observe them, glorify God in the day of visitation.

2:11 **Beloved**. The original word (*agapetos*) means dearly loved, esteemed, favorite and worthy of love. It is closely related to a verb (*agapao*) that means to be well pleased or fond of or contented. This word captures God's heart for you. Your heavenly Father is fond of you. You are his esteemed favorite and he is well pleased with you. He looks at you with a feeling of deep contentment knowing that you are his dearly loved child.

I urge you. If Peter was preaching old covenant law he would say, "I command you..." But since he is preaching new covenant grace, he urges, implores, and exhorts us to make the life-giving choice.

Aliens and strangers. Since you are a citizen of a heavenly kingdom (Php. 3:20), don't act as though you belong to the fallen kingdoms of this world.

Abstain. A preacher of works twists these words into a fitness test. "You have to abstain and avoid sin to purify your soul and make yourself pleasing and acceptable to God." But that is not how Peter does it. Having established your secure identity (you are a chosen race, a royal priesthood and a holy nature; see 1 Pet. 2:9), he begins to address your behavior, and he does this in a most gracious way. "I urge you." In the new covenant, behavior always follows identity.

Fleshly lusts are natural desires as opposed to spiritual desires. Some examples of destructive desires are listed in 1 Peter 2:1 and 4:3.

Wage war. When we feed our flesh, but neglect our spirits, our souls wither.

The desires of the self-life are inherently destructive. Just as the wages of sin is death (Rom. 6:23), the fruit of the flesh is corruption (Gal. 6:8). A mind focused on the preservation of self can never fully experience the abundant life that God offers through his Spirit (Rom. 8:6).

Against the soul. The lusts of the flesh wage war against our purified souls (1 Pet. 1:22).

Your born-again soul does not want to sin (1 John 3:9). When you were born again, you were given a new nature with new desires to please the Lord. This is why the former lusts of the flesh wage war against you. They are not on your side. The devil would love for you to reclaim ownership of those old habits, but a better response is to die to sin and live for righteousness (1 Pet. 2:24).

2:12 **Your behavior**. Live in such a way that others see your good works and praise your Father in heaven (Matt. 5:16). Peter contrasts the good behavior or holy conduct of believers (1 Pet. 1:15, 17, 2:12, 3:1, 8, 16, 2 Pet. 3:11) with the lawless and sensual deeds of the ungodly (1 Pet. 4:3, 2 Pet. 2:7–8, 13–14, 18).

The Gentiles. Unbelievers. Technically a Gentile was a non-Jew or foreigner. But since Peter's letter was sent to churches that had Gentile believers in them (1 Pet. 1:1), he is referring to those outside the church.

Slander. False accusations may seem relatively benign, but historically they have been used by the enemies of the church to great effect. In New Testament times religious Jews falsely accused Christians of being opposed to Caesar. "They're godless heretics who stir up trouble all over the world" (see Acts 17:6–7, 21:28). By spreading slander, they hoped to stir up civil unrest and provoke the Romans into taking action against Christians.

In Corinth, the Jews brought Paul into the Roman courts on the charge of persuading men to worship God in ways contrary to Jewish law (Acts 18:12–13). On that occasion the Roman proconsul did not take the bait. But there were times when the Jews played the Romans like fiddles (e.g., Acts 21:27ff).

Your good deeds are the things you do when you have been apprehended by the goodness of God.

Since the time of Christ, Christians have been at the forefront of the arts and sciences. Christian trailblazers promoted education, built hospitals, created industries, freed slaves, and defended the rights of women and children. Every year, millions of Christians volunteer to feed the poor, visit the sick and imprisoned, and help refugees. Although Christians can be recognized by their good deeds, we are not defined by our good deeds. We are defined by the love of Christ. The good deeds we do are a response to his great love. See also 1 Peter 3:16.

Glorify God. Those unbelievers who are slandering you may yet be won over by your witness and join you in worshipping the Lord when he returns (*cf.* 1 Pet. 4:16).

Visitation. The original word (*episkope*) means inspection. It is the same word that is used to describe the Lord's first coming to Israel in Luke 19:44. In context, "the day of visitation" implies the Lord's final coming or the day of the Lord; see 2 Pet. 3:10.

---

1 Peter 2:13–15

[13] Submit yourselves for the Lord's sake to every human institution,
whether to a king as the one in authority, [14] or to governors as sent
by him for the punishment of evildoers and the praise of those who
do right. [15] For such is the will of God that by doing right you may
silence the ignorance of foolish men.

2:13 **Submit yourselves**. To submit means to yield, defer, and respect. It's something we choose to do in honor of the Lord. Christians are good neighbors and model citizens. When we disagree with those in authority, we disagree respectfully. When we protest, we protest lawfully.

For the Lord's sake. Jesus was no rebel and nor are his followers (Rom. 13:1–2).

Every human institution includes your government, your local council, your workplace, your church, and your school board. Peter is not calling for blind obedience (1 Pet. 2:19), but a respectful and humble attitude.

King or emperor or president or prime minister, etc.

2:14 **Governors**. If we are to honor the king (1 Pet. 2:17), we must respect those who have been sent in his name. The apostle Paul, when unjustly brought before Roman governors, typically spoke with courtesy and respect (e.g., Acts 24:10).

2:15 **The will of God** is one of Peter's favorite phrases (1 Pet. 2:15, 4:2, 6, 19, 5:2). It is God's will for you to honor and pray for those in authority and bear up patiently under unjust suffering (1 Pet. 2:12–14, 20). It is not God's will for you to shoot your mouth off, to rebel, and to act unlike Christ.

Doing right is another one of Peter's favorite phrases (see 1 Pet. 2:20. 3:6, 17, 4:19). In the old covenant, doing right meant keeping the rules, but in the new covenant doing right is what we do when we're living in right relationship with the Creator (1 Pet. 2:24, 4:19).

Silence. We do not silence our enemies by engaging in fruitless debates, but by doing good and by praying for those who persecute us (Matt. 5:44, Rom. 12:18).

The ignorance of foolish men. Those who slander and falsely accuse the body of Christ (see 1 Pet. 2:12).

---

1 Peter 2:16–17

16 Act as free men, and do not use your freedom as a covering for
evil, but use it as bondslaves of God. 17 Honor all people, love the
brotherhood, fear God, honor the king.

2:16 **Act as free men** because in Christ you are free. Let your life be a witness of God's liberating grace. When you submit to your spouse, boss or the king (1 Pet. 2:17, 18, 3:1, 7), do it out of love as a free child of God.

Freedom as a covering for evil. The message of grace has set many people free, but if we use our freedom to rebel or put others down, we've missed the point of grace. Jesus did not set us free from darkness so that we might win arguments or get puffed up with pride. He did it so that we might proclaim the goodness of God and draw others into the Father's loving embrace.

Bondslaves of God. Along with Paul (Rom. 1:1), James (Jas 1:1), and Jude (Jud 1:1), Peter saw himself as a bondslave or bondservant of God (2 Pet 1:1). This can lead to confusion. You may wonder, am I a son or servant of God? You are a son who serves.

Jesus, the Son of God, took on the form of a bondservant (Php. 2:7). He was not confused about his identity – he was God's Son – but he was servant-hearted (Mark 10:45). Jesus was the Son who served.

In the same way, the apostles identified themselves as servants of Christ. They were saying, "We are the sons of God who serve in the manner in which Christ served." Meaning, they served others (2 Cor. 4:5). They did not serve to curry favor with God, but to reveal the Servant-king and win people to Christ. As Paul said, "I have made myself a servant to all, so that I may win more" (1 Cor. 9:19).

It's the same with us. Although we are free in Christ, we willingly serve in the name of Christ so that the orphans and slaves of this world might come to know their Father who loves them. Like Christ, we are the sons who serve.

2:17 **Honor all people**. The world judges people according to their appearance, pedigree, and performance, but we regard no one from a worldly point of view (2 Cor. 5:16). If Jesus died for them, they matter. Everyone is precious to God.

Love the brotherhood. We honor all people, but we show heartfelt and intentional love to our brothers and sisters in the Lord (1 Pet. 1:22). We love one another by clothing ourselves with humility and preferring one another (Rom. 12:10, 1 Pet. 5:5).

Fear God. Worship the Lord, giving him the reverence and honor due his name.

In the old covenant, you were commanded to, "Fear the Lord your God, and serve him only" (Deu. 6:13). But when Jesus quoted this command to the devil, he changed the word *fear* to *worship* (see Matt. 4:10). To fear the Lord in a new covenant sense is to worship him. This sort of fear has nothing to do with pain and punishment but is a proper response to a God who is holy, righteous, awesome, and good.

Honor the king. We respect those in authority regardless of their political persuasions or character flaws.

Some context will help us grasp the significance of these words. Peter lived most of his life under the rule of tyrants. As a Jew, he was governed by the same ruling council (the Sanhedrin) that tried to murder Jesus and which persecuted the early church. As a Galilean who frequently visited Judea, he was subject to the oppressive rule of the Herodians and Roman governors. And as an apostle, he attracted the hostile attention of the emperor Nero, one of history's most wicked rulers.

---

1 Peter 2:18–21

[18] Servants, be submissive to your masters with all respect, not only
to those who are good and gentle, but also to those who are unreasonable. [19] For this finds favor, if for the sake of conscience toward
God a person bears up under sorrows when suffering unjustly. [20] For
what credit is there if, when you sin and are harshly treated, you
endure it with patience? But if when you do what is right and suffer
for it you patiently endure it, this finds favor with God. [21] For you
have been called for this purpose, since Christ also suffered for you,
leaving you an example for you to follow in his steps,

2:18 **Servants... masters**. Respect your boss, even if he's a jerk. It's easy to serve a boss who is good and gentle; it's not so easy if they are unreasonable and demanding. Respect them anyway, says Peter. Serve them as though you were serving the Lord (Eph. 6:7). Pray for them, and in your actions reveal the love of Christ to them.

2:19 **For this finds favor**. Bearing up under unjust treatment is commendable because it shows you are entrusting yourself to the One who judges righteously (1 Pet. 2:23).

The sake of conscience toward God. Sometimes you have to choose between obeying God and human authority.

So far Peter has been encouraging us to submit to kings, unreasonable bosses, and every human institution. But that does not mean we should do things that violate our consciences. When Peter and John were commanded by the Sanhedrin to never teach or even speak about Jesus, they refused (see Acts 4:18–20).

We submit to every human authority as an act of obedience to the Lord. But if those authorities ask us to disobey the Lord and do things that violate our conscience, we respectfully refuse, even if it leads to unjust suffering.

Bears up under sorrows. You patiently endure persecution or unjust suffering (see next verse).

Suffering unjustly. Sometimes obeying God leads to unjust treatment from the very authorities you have been treating with respect.

When the Sanhedrin judged Paul to be a troublemaker, he looked them in the eye and said, "Brethren, I have lived my life with a perfectly good conscience before God up to this day" (Acts 23:1). This sort of behavior is commendable, but it can lead to suffering. Paul was beaten, imprisoned, and ultimately executed for refusing to heed those who tried to silence him.

2:20 **When you sin**. There is nothing commendable about bearing up under punishment that is justly deserved.

Do what is right. Doing what is right means living in right relationship with Jesus the Righteous One. It means you are a believer; see 1 Pet. 2:15.

Suffer. "Suffer for doing what is right" can be read as suffering for the sake of righteousness (1 Pet. 3:14) or suffering for being a Christian (1 Pet. 4:16). It's being persecuted for your faith in Christ.

Patiently endure it. When we are unjustly treated, the flesh reacts with indignation. But Christ, when he was slandered and persecuted, remained silent. He trusted God to work things out (1 Pet. 2:23). When we respond to persecution in the same manner as Christ, our behavior is a witness to others (1 Pet. 3:15–16).

Finds favor with God. The word for *find* should be in italics as it is not in the original text and has been added by translators. Since the word for favor (*charis*) can be translated as grace, a literal reading of this verse is as follows: if you patiently endure, (this is) grace from God. Alternatively, God will give you the grace to patiently endure.

The early Christians were unjustly treated on account of their faith in Christ. They were flogged, imprisoned, and some, including Peter, were martyred. They did not endure because of their intestinal fortitude; they endured because God was with them. In the same way, you will endure your trials when you realize that God is with you and he holds you securely in his hand.

2:21 **Called for this purpose**. This is the life to which we have been called – the life of Christ. It's a blessed life of doing what is good and right and occasionally suffering for it. As strangers in this world and citizens of another kingdom, we swim against the current.

Leaving you an example. Christ's reaction to hostility inspires us. He did not fight back or call down heavenly fire on his enemies, but he laid down his life to show us how much he loves us.

Follow in his steps. Jesus wins people to himself when we reveal his sacrificial love to others.

In this me-first world, there is nothing special about defending your views or attacking those who disagree with you. But when you surrender your rights, love your enemies, and entrust yourself to God, you present the world with a picture of a superior reality, one based on love, forgiveness, and peace.

---

1 Peter 2:22–23

22 "Who committed no sin, nor was any deceit found in his mouth";
23 and while being reviled, he did not revile in return; while suffering,
he uttered no threats, but kept entrusting himself to him who judges
righteously;

2:22 **No sin**. Jesus is the sinless Man from heaven, not born of Adam's line, and the only human who did not grasp, claw, or fight for his rights. He showed us another way to live and then he laid down his sinless life so that we might be free. Because he was without sin, he was able to ransom our lives from sin's captivity.

Deceit. Jesus never said a word he did not mean (the quote is from Is. 53:9). If he had, the Pharisees would have brayed about it and the law teachers would have hung him for it.

We marvel at the Lord's ability to bridle his tongue, as though he was able to refrain from saying what he was thinking. But the Lord's pure speech reflected his pure heart. When you are abiding in the love of the Father, you do not need to watch your words. When you have made God your Source, everything you do and say will be good.

2:23 **Reviled... suffering**. Jesus face hatred and violence and this was not the hatred of social media trolls, but the vitriol of the most powerful men in Israel and their fanatical followers. Jesus was often slandered (e.g., Matt. 11:19) and on several occasions people tried to murder him (Luke 4:29, 13:31, John 5:18, 7:1).

He uttered no threats. The Lord's silence in the face of injustice speaks volumes (Is. 53:7).

When we are unjustly treated, our flesh reacts with indignation. It cries out in self-defence. But Jesus denied himself and put his faith in his Father.

Entrusting himself. In his darkest hour, Jesus put his life in his Father's hands. As the Son of God, he could have called down fire from heaven or summoned angel armies to slaughter those who were trying to kill him. With a word he could have split the planet. But he stayed silent, like a lamb to the slaughter, because he trusted his Father would make things right. In doing this he set an example for us to follow (1 Pet. 2:21).

---

1 Peter 2:24–25

24 and he himself bore our sins in his body on the cross, so that we
might die to sin and live to righteousness; for by his wounds you
were healed. 25 For you were continually straying like sheep, but now
you have returned to the Shepherd and Guardian of your souls.

2:24 **Bore our sins**. Jesus is the Lamb of God who carried away the sins of the whole world (John 1:29). He took responsibility for all our sins so that we might be free from that unbearable burden and be reconciled to God.

Die to sin. So that we might be done with sin once and for all. Jesus broke the prison of sin and secured your freedom. So be free and have nothing to do with your old master sin. Stop acting like the prisoner you once were and enjoy the righteous life that Christ has given you. Reckon yourself dead to sin and alive to God in Christ Jesus (Rom. 6:11).

Live to righteousness. To live to righteousness is to live in right relationship with God. It's living out of your union with the Lord and experiencing life as it was meant to be. It is knowing and being known; loving and being loved. It is being holy because you are holy. It is seeing the touch of God in everything you do and in everyone you meet.

By his wounds you were healed. Our healing is described in the past tense because all the grace we need to live healed and whole was provided at the cross.

When we pray for healing, we do not need to ask God to provide. Rather, we receive what he has made available to us through his Son. We don't pray like beggars asking God to do what he has done; we pray like commanders resisting the devil and all his filthy diseases. To pray with faith means thanking Jesus for the cross and for the healing that is ours in his Name.

2:25 **Straying like sheep**. At one time we were restless wanderers in need of a shepherd. Like sheep, we had all gone astray (Is. 53:6).

The Shepherd. Jesus is the Good Shepherd who calls his sheep by name, watches over them, and lays down his life for them (John 10:11, Heb. 13:20). You can be confident that the Good Shepherd will bring you safely to his heavenly kingdom (2 Tim. 4:18).

The original word for shepherd (*poimen*) can be translated as pastor (Eph. 4:11). Jesus is not just a pastor, he is *the* Pastor, and what a wonderful pastor he is!

Guardian. The Good Shepherd lovingly watches over your soul. He who saves you, keeps you and protects you through the power of God (Ps. 121:5, 145:20).

The original word for guardian (*episkopos*) is translated elsewhere as bishop or overseer (Acts 20:28, 1 Tim. 3:2), which is why some translations say Jesus is the Bishop or Overseer of your souls.

---

1 Peter 3

1 Peter 3:1–4

[1] In the same way, you wives, be submissive to your own husbands so that even if any of them are disobedient to the word, they may be won without a word by the behavior of their wives, [2] as they observe your chaste and respectful behavior. [3] Your adornment must not be merely external—braiding the hair, and wearing gold jewelry, or putting on dresses; [4] but let it be the hidden person of the heart, with the imperishable quality of a gentle and quiet spirit, which is precious in the sight of God.

3:1 **In the same way** that Christ gave us an example to follow by laying down his life for us (see 1 Pet. 2:21), husbands and wives are to yield and lay down their lives for each other. Speaking first to wives and then to husbands (see 1 Pet. 3:7), Peter encourages both to submit to each other in love.

Be submissive. Putting the needs of the other first is the essence of love. "Love is not self-seeking" (1 Cor. 13:5). We give ourselves to those we love as an act of worship to the One who gave himself for us.

True submission stems from love, not power. It is saying, "Because I love you, I choose to put you first." Submission is not forced on us from above; it is something we offer to another. It's choosing to surrender because we want to, not because we have to.

Disobedient to the word. Unbelievers (1 Pet. 2:8).

In a healthy marriage, wives submit to husbands, husbands submit to wives, and both submit to Christ (Eph. 5:21). But what if the husband is an unbeliever? What can the Christian wife do then? She can follow the lead of Queen Esther who won her husband with sacrificial love. A believing wife is a priest in her marriage. Through her loving deeds and gentle speech, she may lead her man to righteousness.

They may be won for the Lord.

If your husband is an unbeliever, don't write him off or settle for a second-rate marriage. Own the situation. Step up and take the lead. Pray for your husband. In your actions, reveal the unconditional love of the Father to him. Don't love him more when he goes to church or less when he doesn't. Unconditional love is winsome and it can melt hard hearts.

Without a word. We can win people for Jesus through our loving actions.

3:2 **Chaste** means innocent, modest, and pure.

Respectful. The original word (*phobos*) means fear, but the translation fits the context. A wise woman does not try to dominate or manipulate her husband. Instead, she listens and defers to him with genuine love and respect.

Behavior. Actions speak louder than words.

3:3 **Not merely external**. True beauty comes from a heart that is established in the love of the Lord (see next verse). What you wear or don't wear is a secondary concern.

3:4 **The hidden person**. The inner you (your spirit and soul), which endures, can be contrasted with the outer you (your mortal body), which fades away.

Imperishable quality. Our physical appearance will age, but true godliness lasts forever.

A gentle and quiet spirit is meek like Jesus (Matt. 21:5). Being meek does not mean being a pushover. Meekness is the attitude that accompanies faith in God.

Precious in the sight of God. God is more interested in your heart than your hairdo (see 1 Sam. 16:7).

---

1 Peter 3:5–6

[5] For in this way in former times the holy women also, who hoped in God, used to adorn themselves, being submissive to their own husbands; [6] just as Sarah obeyed Abraham, calling him lord, and you have become her children if you do what is right without being frightened by any fear.

3:5 **In former times**. In the Old Testament, godly women won over their husbands through gentleness and respect rather than external adornments and nagging. Esther is the stand-out example. "If it pleases the king..." (Est. 5:4). With five words and a gentle spirit, Esther turned the heart of her foolish husband.

3:6 **Sarah obeyed Abraham**. Abraham occasionally made some bad life choices but his wife stood with him through thick and thin.

Peter has been discussing godly wives submitting to unbelieving husbands (see 1 Pet. 3:1). Strangely the example he chooses is a man revered for being the father of the faith. But even good men miss the way from time to time, and Abraham was no exception. He pretended his wife was his sister and allowed her to be taken into Pharaoh's household (Gen. 12:11–15), and then he repeated his deception with Abimelech (Gen. 20:2). Yet even when Abraham acted foolishly, Sarah never called him a fool. She remained a faithful partner for better or worse.

Calling him lord (see Gen 18:12). The point is not that Sarah served Abraham in the way a servant serves a master, but that she submitted to him in the way a loving wife (or husband) submits to her husband (or wife). A wife may refer to her husband as "my king," and a husband may refer to his wife as "my queen." But both do so out of love and affection rather than coercion and control.

You have become her children. Just as Abraham is the spiritual father of all who have faith in God (see Gal. 3:7), Sarah is the spiritual mother of those who follow her godly example.

If you do what is right. If you choose to love with the unconditional love that God has for you.

Equality and mutual respect are essential ingredients of a healthy marriage, but equality is never the goal; love is. A good marriage is a partnership between equals who don't see themselves as equal. The husband loves his wife more than his own life, and the wife submits to her husband as to the Lord. Each prefers the other to themselves.

Without being frightened. Let your actions be motivated by the love of Christ, rather than the fear of man. There is no fear in perfect love, but there will be fear if your spouse is threatening, abusive or violent. The exhortation to be submissive should not be read as "let him (or her) mistreat you." But as God has given you grace, sow grace into your marriage.

---

1 Peter 3:7

7 You husbands in the same way, live with your wives in an understanding way, as with someone weaker, since she is a woman; and show her honor as a fellow heir of the grace of life, so that your prayers will not be hindered.

3:7 **You husbands in the same way**. As Sarah obeyed and submitted to Abraham, husbands are to submit to and obey their wives.

Love is other-focused. Love trusts, obeys, and yields. Some men are familiar with the verse about wives submitting to their husbands, but they miss the bit where Peter says, "You submit too." Or they rewrite his words. "Wives submit to husbands, while husbands merely honor their wives." That won't fly. "In the same way," means *in the same way*. Whatever submission is expected of the wife is also expected of the husband. As Paul said to husbands and wives, "Submit to one another out of reverence for Christ (Eph. 5:21). Love is a two-way street.

As with someone weaker. The original word for someone (*skeuos*) means vessel or container, and this is how the word is usually translated. "Honor the woman as the weaker vessel." Husbands need to treat their wives with the same care as they would handle a valuable piece of pottery, not because she is fragile, but because she is precious and deserving of respect.

Peter is not saying females are feeble or more easily upset. The suggestion that women are in some way inferior to men stems from an ancient prejudice, but it was not one that Peter shared.

Every time he went to the Temple, Peter passed through the outer Women's Court on his way to the male-only Court of Israel. Every time he attended the synagogue or saw a woman get stoned for adultery, Peter was reminded that women have not had a fair shake. From the day women were born, their rights were weaker, and their prospects bleaker. Taking his lead from Jesus, Peter spoke out against this injustice. He encouraged women to prophesy and speak as though speaking the very words of God (1 Pet. 4:11). He treated women with respect, and he instructed husbands to treat their wives as fellow heirs of grace.

Weaker. Science tells us that women have better immune systems, better genes, and they live longer than men. They experience less stress and lower heart disease, and are much less likely to start wars. Companies run by women are more profitable, countries led by women do better at surviving pandemics, and women perform better academically (when given the chance). Women are surely different, but it's inaccurate to say they are weaker. Yet many men think women are weaker, and this is the mindset that Peter is addressing. It's not his view, but *their* view, and this is why their prayers are hindered.

Show her honor. The original word for honor (*time*) means precious value (1 Pet. 2:7). It's the same word that describes how God honors the Son (2 Pet. 1:17) and believers value the Lord (1 Pet. 2:7). While we may debate how women are weaker, there is no question that husbands are to honor their wives as highly-valued and equal in grace.

A fellow heir. If you see yourself as superior to others, you are not walking in grace.

That wives were fellow heirs would have been a radical notion for first-century men. Even today some have trouble accepting their wives as equal partners in the Lord. Those who dismiss their wives as weaker or subordinate, will find their prayers hindered.

Heir of the grace of life. Life is God's gracious gift to humanity, and women have just as much of a share in it as men. This is especially true when it comes to the gift of eternal life.

So that your prayers will not be hindered. The prayers which are hindered are those that begin, "Thank God that I am not like other people" (Luke 18:11).

If you look down on your spouse or others, your prayer life will be impeded by your own infernal pride. You will have trouble receiving grace because your haughty heart has no room for it. You may not say it in so many words, but your attitude is, "*They* need grace, but I don't." Since your heart is in the wrong place, it will seem like heaven is closed to your prayers and God is resisting you (see 1 Pet. 5:5).

---

1 Peter 3:8–9

[8] To sum up, all of you be harmonious, sympathetic, brotherly, kind-
hearted, and humble in spirit; [9] not returning evil for evil or insult for
insult, but giving a blessing instead; for you were called for the very
purpose that you might inherit a blessing.

3:8 **To sum up**. The secret to happy and healthy relationships is not complicated.

Be harmonious. Be like-minded.

In any marriage, church, or organization there will be a diversity of viewpoints. Having harmony requires a commitment to compassion and love that exceeds any differences of opinion. Putting others first means hearing what they say and feeling what they feel. It's choosing to love and support them even if you do not love and support their viewpoint.

Sympathetic. Compassionate.

Brotherly. Treat believers like family.

Humble in spirit. Where there is humility, there is harmony. Where there is selfish ambition, there are quarrels and strife and all sorts of trouble (Jas. 3:16).

3:9 **Not returning evil for evil**. Any relationship that is based on keeping score is doomed. But a relationship that keeps no record of wrongs will endure any storm.

Insult for insult. Trading insults is a fast track to discord and strife. Instead of repaying in kind, follow Christ's lead and repay with kindness (Luke 6:27–29).

Giving a blessing instead. Sow what you want to reap. "Treat others the same way you want them to treat you" (Luke 6:31). Paul said something similar (Rom. 12:17, 1 Thess. 5:15).

You were called. When God called you out of darkness (1 Pet. 2:9), it was for the purpose of including you in his family so that you might become an heir and inherit a blessing.

Inherit a blessing. In Christ we are heirs of salvation (Heb. 1:14), heirs of eternal life (Matt. 19:29, Eph. 1:14, Tit. 3:7), and heirs of a blessed and gracious life (Eph. 1:3, 1 Pet. 3:7, 9). In him, we are heirs of all things (John 17:10, Heb. 1:2).

---

1 Peter 3:10–12

10 For, "The one who desires life, to love and see good days, must
keep his tongue from evil and his lips from speaking deceit. 11 He
must turn away from evil and do good; he must seek peace and pursue it. 12 "For the eyes of the Lord are toward the righteous, and his
ears attend to their prayer, but the face of the Lord is against those
who do evil."

3:10 **Life**. The secret to a long and happy life is to pursue peace, and Jesus is the Prince of Peace (Is. 9:6). When we proclaim the gospel of peace (Eph. 6:15), we are revealing the way of peace (Luke 1:79), which leads us to the God of peace (Rom. 15:33), who gives us life and peace (Rom. 8:6).

Keep his tongue from evil. Someone with an old covenant mindset reads these words (from Psalm 34:12–14) as a collection of aphorisms and life hacks. "If you want a good life, learn to control your tongue." But the tongue cannot be tamed (Jas. 3:8). The tongue is a restless evil, and all the effort in the world cannot cure it. Only the Holy Spirit can give us a new heart, a new tongue, and a new life.

The divine life that God offers is more than a collection of tips and tricks. The Christian life is the Prince of Peace living in us. Abide in Christ, and everything you say and do will be good.

3:11 **Do good**. In the old covenant, doing good meant keeping the rules; but in the new covenant, doing good is what we do when we experience the goodness of God.

When Jesus said, "*Those who have done good* will rise to live" (John 5:28–29), he was speaking in the context of walking by faith in him (see John 5:24). Similarly, when Paul said God will give eternal life to *those who persist in doing good*, he meant the same thing (Rom. 2:6–7). Doing good in a spiritual sense is living in union with the One who is good, and allowing his goodness to flow through us to others.

Peace is something to pursue, and in Christ you have it.

The kingdom of God is righteousness, peace, and joy in the Holy Spirit (Rom. 14:17). If the message you're listening to doesn't reveal Jesus and the gift of his righteousness, you will never experience the peace and joy that comes with it. But if you receive the righteousness that comes by faith, you will be satisfied, content, and enjoy peace with God.

3:12 **The eyes of the Lord**. Peter quotes an Old Testament scripture (2 Chr. 16:9) to make a new covenant point: The Lord is watching over you and he hears your prayers (1 Pet. 1:5; 1 John 5:15). You don't need to fast and pray to get the Lord's attention. His face is already shining upon you with love.

The righteous are those who have humbled themselves before God and have received, by faith, the free gift of his righteousness. When the Lord looks at the believer, he sees someone who is 100 percent righteous.

The Lord is against, or opposed to, the haughty and self-righteous. An old covenant mindset reads this as, "The Lord hates sinners," but Jesus is the friend of sinners. It is not the broken sinner he opposes, but those who are proud and see no need for grace (1 Pet. 5:5).

Those who do evil are the proud and ungodly who show contempt for God's kindness (Rom. 2:2–5). They resist his Spirit and scorn the Son who might otherwise save them (2 Pet. 2:5).

---

1 Peter 3:13–17

[13] Who is there to harm you if you prove zealous for what is good?
[14] But even if you should suffer for the sake of righteousness, you are blessed. "And do not fear their intimidation, and do not be troubled,"
[15] but sanctify Christ as Lord in your hearts, always being ready to make a defense to everyone who asks you to give an account for the hope that is in you, yet with gentleness and reverence;
[16] and keep a good conscience so that in the thing in which you are slandered, those who revile your good behavior in Christ will be put to shame.
[17] For it is better, if God should will it so, that you suffer for doing what is right rather than for doing what is wrong.

3:13 **Who is there to harm you?** Why should you experience trouble if you are enthusiastic in serving the Lord? Christians make good citizens (1 Pet. 2:13).

What is good. God is good (Mark 10:18). To be zealous for what is good is to be passionate about the goodness of God. It's being so full of your Father's love that you want others to experience his goodness too.

3:14 To **suffer for the sake of righteousness** is to suffer for being a Christian (1 Pet. 4:16). Trials and tribulations are a normal part of the Christian life (2 Tim. 3:12).

You are blessed because God is in your corner; your persecution proves it. If you belonged to the world, you would not be suffering for the sake of righteousness. You are a citizen of an eternal kingdom. Your unjust and temporary afflictions are evidence of that.

Do not fear. The children of God can face trials and tribulations without fear because they know God has the last word

(Jas. 5:8–9). No matter what happens, the Risen Lord is mighty to save.

Intimidation. The original noun (*phobos*) is related to the verb fear (*phobeo*), so Peter is saying the same thing as Isaiah 8:12: "Do not fear what they fear." When trials come, the unbeliever has no choice but to fear. But when you are resting in the Lord, your heart will be untroubled and you will smile at the storm (John 14:1, 27).

3:15 **Sanctify Christ as Lord in your hearts**. Honor Jesus as the Lord of your situation.

When you are suffering through trials or afflictions, the temptation is to think that God doesn't know and doesn't care. But the Guardian of your soul is watching over you, and his power protects you (1 Pet. 1:5, 3:12).

To say, "Jesus is Lord," is to declare, "He is greater than what I am going through." It is having the confidence that he will bring you safely to the other side (Is. 41:10).

Being ready. What looks like persecution may actually be an opportunity to reveal the love of God to those who are attacking you (1 Pet. 2:21).

Defense. Be ready to explain why you have hope in a hopeless situation. Be ready to talk about the Risen Lord who gives life and hope to those who are as good as dead (1 Pet. 1:3).

The hope that is in you. If faith is the confidence we have for today, hope is the confidence we have for tomorrow. Jesus is the Source of our faith and hope, and is the reason we can be fearless in the face of death (Rev. 2:10).

3:16 **Keep a good conscience**. Don't let lies and false accusations get to you.

Walk in grace and you will be accused of being anti-law and pro-sin. You will be dismissed as extreme, unbalanced, or *hyper*-grace, as though that were a bad thing. Heed these accusations and you risk casting away your good conscience and shipwrecking your faith (1 Tim. 1:18–19). The best response to slander is to reassure your heart that your heavenly Father knows you and loves you (1 John 3:20–21). If God justifies you, who can condemn you (Rom. 8:31–33)?

Conscience. The conscience makes judgments based on knowledge, and the most reliable source of knowledge is the Spirit of Truth. When the Holy Spirit bears witness with our spirits that *this is the way to go*, and your conscience heeds this instruction, your conscience will be good and clear.

Slandered; see 1 Pet. 2:12.

Your good behavior in Christ. Good behavior is what you display when you have been apprehended by the goodness of God. Anyone can do good deeds, but good deeds *in Christ* are what you do when you are living from your union with Jesus the Righteous One and are living for righteousness (1 Pet. 2:24).

Put to shame. When the truth comes out, those who slandered you will be embarrassed over the shoddy way they treated you.

3:17 **If God should will it**. Some read these words as though God was the cause of their suffering. "God gave me this trial to teach me character." But the context is *unjust* suffering for the sake of righteousness (1 Pet. 3:14). Why would God persecute you for being a Christian? Why would a good God punish those who do right?

A just God cannot author unjust suffering, and it is not his will for his children to be abused or mistreated. God redeems our suffering; he doesn't cause it.

If the wrong way to read this verse is, "Sometimes it is God's will for you to suffer persecution," what is the right way to read it? Peter is saying the same thing he says in the next chapter where he talks about suffering for doing God's will. He's talking about being persecuted for being a Christian (see 1 Pet. 4:19).

Suffer for doing what is right. It is better to suffer for being a Christian than to suffer for being a criminal (1 Pet. 4:15–16).

Doing what is right; see 1 Pet. 2:15.

Doing what is wrong; see 1 Pet. 4:15

1 Peter 3:18–20

[18] For Christ also died for sins once for all, the just for the unjust, so
that he might bring us to God, having been put to death in the flesh,
but made alive in the spirit; [19] in which also he went and made proclamation to the spirits now in prison, [20] who once were disobedient,
when the patience of God kept waiting in the days of Noah, during
the construction of the ark, in which a few, that is, eight persons,
were brought safely through the water.

3:18 **Died for sins once for all**. All our sins – past, present, and future – were dealt with, once and for all time, at the cross (Heb. 10:12). God doesn't do partial redemptions. On the cross, Jesus took away the sins of the whole world and no further sacrifice for sin remains (Heb. 9:26, 10:18, 1 John 2:2).

The just for the unjust. God justifies the ungodly (Rom. 4:5). This is the astonishing announcement of grace. Whether you are a good sinner or a bad sinner or the worst sinner who ever lived, God has done everything to make things right, and if you accept that with humility and thanksgiving, you are 100 percent right with God.

In the flesh. In the body.

Made alive in the spirit. Jesus was raised to life by the Holy Spirit (Rom. 8:11).

3:19 **The spirits now in prison**. Those who are dead. It seems Jesus, after he died and was buried, went and preached to those who had died before him.

Although the prophets glimpsed God's plan for salvation (1 Pet. 1:10), most Old Testament people had no idea what was coming (Heb. 9:8). Since they died without hearing the gospel, how could they obey the gospel? Someone had to tell them, and it seems that Jesus did (see Eph. 4:9). But this is far from certain.

Some say that Jesus went and preached to fallen angels, but the angels who abandoned heaven are being confined in darkness until Judgment Day (Jude 1:6). It seems more likely that the imprisoned spirits refer to people, and Peter seems to confirm this (see 1 Pet. 4:6).

Made proclamation. He announced, or declared, the good news (1 Pet. 1:12).

Prison. The context suggests that the prison is the grave – Sheol in Hebrew, or Hades in Greek. It is the abode of the dead and should not be confused with Hell.

3:20 **Who once were disobedient**. Dead unbelievers (1 Pet. 4:6), including those who were destroyed in the time of Noah (2 Pet. 2:5).

The patience of God kept waiting. The God who is not willing that any perish (2 Pet. 3:9) waited for the ancients to repent.

The days of Noah. Noah, the heir of righteousness, condemned the ancient world (Heb. 11:7); Jesus, the king of righteousness, showed them the way of righteousness so that they might be saved.

Eight persons. Noah, his wife, their three sons and their wives were saved through the flood (Gen. 7:13).

---

1 Peter 3:21–22

21 Corresponding to that, baptism now saves you—not the removal
of dirt from the flesh, but an appeal to God for a good conscience—
through the resurrection of Jesus Christ, 22 who is at the right hand
of God, having gone into heaven, after angels and authorities and
powers had been subjected to him.

3:21 **Corresponding to that**. Noah's salvation through water is a prophetic picture of spiritual baptism.

Baptism now saves you. The baptism that saves is the baptism done to every believer by the Holy Spirit. The moment you came to Jesus, you were baptized, or placed, into his body by the Holy Spirit (1 Cor. 12:12–13). This is the *one* baptism that counts (Eph. 4:5).

Appeal. The original word (*eperotema*) means inquiry or question. It can also mean earnest seeking or demand. It does not mean answer or pledge (as some translations have it). When we make a sincere appeal for salvation – "God, have mercy on me" – God responds with an immediate action. He baptizes us into Christ's death and raises us with Christ and seats us in heavenly places (Eph. 2:6). "We have been buried with him through baptism into death, so that as Christ was raised from the dead through the glory of the Father, so we too might walk in newness of life" (Rom. 6:4).

A good conscience is what you have when you are walking in step with the Holy Spirit (Rom. 9:1).

Through the resurrection of Jesus Christ. Jesus is not a dead savior of no use to anyone; he is the Risen Savior who saves to the uttermost (Heb. 7:25).

3:22 **At the right hand of God**. The Son shares his Father's throne (Matt. 22:44, Heb. 10:12).

Having gone into heaven. Jesus is no longer in the grave but has returned to heaven in triumph with "captives" (Old Testament saints) in his train (Eph. 4:8).

Authorities and powers. Who are the authorities and powers that influence the affairs of men? We do not need to know. All that should concern us is that all angels and authorities and powers are subject to King Jesus. To be effective in prayer, we only need to lift up the Name that is above all other names.

Subjected to him. The One who was despised and rejected by men has been made Lord of all, even if we don't see it yet (Heb. 2:8).

---

1 Peter 4

1 Peter 4:1–2

1 Therefore, since Christ has suffered in the flesh, arm yourselves also
with the same purpose, because he who has suffered in the flesh has
ceased from sin, 2 so as to live the rest of the time in the flesh no
longer for the lusts of men, but for the will of God.

4:1 **Suffered in the flesh… in the flesh**. Jesus suffered physical pain and death in his body.

Arm yourselves also with the same purpose. Have the same mindset as Christ when it comes to sin.

Has ceased from sin. Whoever has died is done with sin. Satan wants you to think that you have no choice when it comes to sin. "I have a sinful nature. I can't help what I do." But the old person you used to be was crucified with Christ (Rom. 6:6–7). You don't have a sinful nature. In union with the Lord, you have the nature of Christ himself (2 Pet. 1:4). So reckon yourself dead to sin and live for God (Rom 6:11).

4:2 **Live the rest of the time in the flesh**. For as long as you live in your earthly body.

The lusts of men, or the lusts of the flesh, are the desires of the unspiritual life. Peter gives some examples of fleshly desires in 1 Peter 2:1 and 4:3.

The will of God is for you to walk in newness of life by trusting in his Son Jesus (John 6:40, Rom. 6:4). As a slave of sin you had no choice but to walk in the flesh (see next verse). Having been redeemed with the precious blood of Jesus (1 Pet. 1:18–19), you can now walk in the new way of the spirit.

---

1 Peter 4:3–6

3 For the time already past is sufficient for you to have carried out
the desire of the Gentiles, having pursued a course of sensuality,
lusts, drunkenness, carousing, drinking parties and abominable ido-
latries. 4 In all this, they are surprised that you do not run with them

into the same excesses of dissipation, and they malign you; [5] but they will give account to him who is ready to judge the living and the dead. [6] For the gospel has for this purpose been preached even to those who are dead, that though they are judged in the flesh as men, they may live in the spirit according to the will of God.

4:3 **The time already past**. You've spent enough time living the self-destructive life of the flesh.

The desire of the Gentiles. What unbelievers like to do.

Sensuality. To pursue a course of sensuality is to walk after the flesh without any regard for the things of God. It's living in response to your natural appetites, leaning on your strengths (your abilities and understanding), and living solely from the basis of your earthly experience (what you see, hear, touch, know, etc.). The sensual life of independence can be contrasted with the spiritual life of reliance on God.

Lusts, etc. The desires of the flesh are revealed in various deeds of the flesh (Gal. 5:19–21).

4:4 **They are surprised**. Those who live in the flesh marvel that you no longer follow them down that self-destructive path. Blind to their bondage, they cannot understand why you no longer join them in their revelries.

Excesses of dissipation. The mindless wastefulness of that corrupt and empty lifestyle.

They malign you. They mock and revile you.

4:5 **Give account**. Those who mock you will have to explain themselves before the judgment seat of God (Rom. 14:10).

Peter sees two outcomes for those who malign and mock Christians. Some will have to give the Lord a "please explain" for their poor conduct, while others will repent and join you in glorifying the Lord when he returns (1 Pet. 2:12).

The living and the dead. Everyone is judged, including those who are dead at the time of Christ's return (Acts 10:42, 2 Tim. 4:1, Rev. 20:12–13).

The prospect of judgment should not frighten the believer. One with the Lord, his future is your future. You can look forward to Judgment Day with confidence (1 John 4:17).

4:6 **This purpose**. Because the dead are judged (see previous verse), they need to hear the gospel.

Those who are dead. Those who died prior to the cross; see 1 Pet. 3:19.

Judged in the flesh as men. They died. The sentence of death came to them (1 Cor. 15:22).

They may live in the spirit as born-again believers and children of God. We are all called to live in the spirit, but here Peter is talking about "those who are dead," meaning people who died prior to the coming of Jesus Christ. Although they died, they yet may be clothed with resurrection bodies as all believers are (1 Cor. 15:52, Php. 3:21).

The will of God is for none to perish and all to repent. (2 Pet. 3:9). How does this apply to those who perished before the cross? How could the dead put their faith in the Risen Lord before the Lord rose? Either they had a prophetic understanding of what was to come (1 Pet. 1:10), or Someone had to visit them in the grave and tell them the good news (1 Pet. 3:19).

---

1 Peter 4:7–9

7 The end of all things is near; therefore, be of sound judgment and
sober spirit for the purpose of prayer. 8 Above all, keep fervent in
your love for one another, because love covers a multitude of sins.
9 Be hospitable to one another without complaint.

4:7 **The end of all things** refers to the end of the age, the end of sin, Judgment Day, and the glorious return of the Lord to earth.

Peter did not know when the Son of Man would return (Matt. 24:36), yet he and the other apostles understood by the Holy

Spirit that they were living in the last days. We continue to live in the last days, and the end of all things is nearer than ever (Heb. 1:2).

Sound judgment. Live intentionally with the end in mind. Don't waste your life, but live with purpose.

Sober spirit. Don't be so consumed with your appetites that you never give a moment's thought to the Lord's return. Live with eternity in mind (1 Pet. 1:13).

Prayer is an appropriate activity for those who are watchful and awaiting the Lord's return. Prayer is conversing with your heavenly Father. A healthy prayer life will include: praising the Lord and giving thanks for all he has done (Acts 16:25, Col. 1:12, 3:17), praying for others, including those in authority (Eph. 1:16, 1 Tim. 2:1), and presenting your requests to God (Php. 4:6, 1 John 5:14–15).

4:8 **Fervent**. The original word (*ektenes*) means intent (as in intentional), earnest, and constant. True love is not a feeling but a decision. It is choosing to humble ourselves and prefer one another (1 Pet. 5:5). It's laying down our rights, our agendas, and our lives as Christ laid down his life for us (John 15:13). Such a love cannot be manufactured from within. It can only be received and passed on from the One who is the Source of love (1 John 4:19).

One another. Fellow believers.

Love covers a multitude of sins. To cover or hide the sins of others is to choose to not see their sins. "Love overlooks the mistakes of others" (Pro. 17:9, TPT).

Although there are times when love compels us to confront the hurts that have been done to us by others (e.g., Matt. 18:15), we are not the sin-police. We are not to set ourselves up as little judges (Jas. 4:11). Our part is to love our brothers and sisters and stick with them through thick and thin.

When Jesus came to earth, he did not go around finding fault and pointing out our sin. He just loved us despite our faults. Go and do likewise.

4:9 **Be hospitable**. Give yourself to others. Open your heart and your home to your brothers and sisters (Rom. 12:13).

When we open our hearts to the love of God, we find the doors of our hearts opening to people. Jesus was a people-person. As we allow him to express his love in our lives, we become people-*people* too.

Without complaint. Do it cheerfully and out of love. Don't offer meals and beds because you have to; do it because we're family.

---

1 Peter 4:10–11

10 As each one has received a special gift, employ it in serving one
another as good stewards of the manifold grace of God. 11 Whoever
speaks, is to do so as one who is speaking the utterances of God; whoever serves is to do so as one who is serving by the strength which God supplies; so that in all things God may be glorified through Jesus Christ, to whom belongs the glory and dominion forever and ever. Amen.

4:10 **Each one has received a special gift**. Every believer has been graced by God with spiritual gifts for the purpose of building the church (1 Cor. 12:7, 14:12).

Employ it. Put your gift to work. You may think that you need a special qualification before you can serve, or that you are disqualified by your gender or pedigree, but Peter says no such thing. You are qualified by the Lord. The grace of God that empowered the apostles empowers you (Rom. 12:6).

Good stewards. One way to tell if we are being good stewards of God's grace is that the exercise of our gifts and talents results in praise to our heavenly Father (Matt. 5:16).

Manifold grace means God's grace comes in a variety of flavors. The original word for manifold (*poikilos*) means motley and is suggestive of a "many-colored tapestry" (to quote the Passion Translation). Just as it is a mistake to limit God, it's a mistake to think his gifts and grace conform to traditional ministry types. For every problem and need, the Creator has a creative and life-giving solution.

Grace of God; see 1 Pet. 5:5.

4:11 **Whoever speaks**. We have all been called to proclaim the goodness of God (Mark 16:15, Heb. 5:12). Note that some older translations say, "If any man speak," giving the impression that only men can speak in church. However, the original text is gender neutral. If Peter had believed women should not speak, preach, teach, or prophesy, this would have been the perfect time to say so.

As a Jewish man, Peter had been raised under the law-keeping covenant. The old covenant was racist (Gentiles are unclean) and sexist (women are inferior), but the new covenant is neither. After being with Jesus, Peter understood that racial and gender distinctions are irrelevant to the ministry of the Spirit (Gal. 3:28). Peter calls us to speak and serve (1 Pet. 2:9, 3:7, 15, 4:11), and not once does he rule out women. If God has gifted you to speak, then speak as though you're speaking the very words of God, and let no one silence you.

The utterances of God. If God has gifted you to speak, then speak boldly and don't hold back. Don't let timidity or the voice of condemnation cause you to stay silent.

Whoever serves. It is the grace of God that qualifies you to serve in his name.

The strength which God supplies. Whatever you do, do it in the strength and power of the Lord.

Rely on your own strength (your natural abilities and understanding), and you will be fruitless and worn out (Jer. 17:5–6). But those who lean on the Lord's strength and direction will be rested, blessed, and very fruitful (Jer. 17:7–8).

Supplies. The original word (*choregeo*) means to pay for the chorus. In Greek festivals and plays, a wealthy patron would fund the performance of live music. They would hire, train, and dress the performers. Similarly, the God who has called and gifted you to shine will train, dress, and provide you with everything you need to deliver a performance worthy of his name.

In all things God may be glorified through Jesus Christ. Whatever you do, do it for the glory of God. Don't do it to make a name for yourself. Do it to make Jesus famous.

Glory and dominion forever. Peter is quoting a doxology, or praise prayer, that was known in the New Testament church (Rev. 1:6, 5:13).

---

1 Peter 4:12–14

12 Beloved, do not be surprised at the fiery ordeal among you, which
comes upon you for your testing, as though some strange thing were
happening to you; 13 but to the degree that you share the sufferings
of Christ, keep on rejoicing, so that also at the revelation of his glory
you may rejoice with exultation. 14 If you are reviled for the name of
Christ, you are blessed, because the Spirit of glory and of God rests
on you.

4:12 **The fiery ordeal among you**. The church was experiencing a time of severe persecution (1 Pet. 4:17).

For your testing. The trials of life reveal your true identity. If you are being persecuted for your faith, it means you have been recognized as one of God's children. You should consider this a blessing and not something to be ashamed of (1 Pet. 4:14, 16).

As though some strange thing were happening to you. We should not be surprised when trials come. Jesus warned that we would be hated on account of his Name (Matt. 10:22). "If they persecuted me, they will also persecute you" (John 15:20).

4:13 **Share the sufferings**. Jesus Christ faced persecution. We share in his sufferings if we are persecuted for being a Christian (1 Pet. 4:16).

Keep on rejoicing. To be persecuted on account of your faith in Christ means that you remind the world of Jesus, and that's something to celebrate.

When we are persecuted on account of Christ, we are to "rejoice and be glad," said Jesus, "for great is your reward in heaven" (Matt. 5:12). The reward we get is the honor of being numbered among the prophets who were also persecuted.

Peter preached what he practiced. After he and John were flogged and released from their sham trial before the Sanhedrin, they left "rejoicing that they had been considered worthy to suffer shame for his name" (Acts 5:41).

At the revelation of his glory. When the Lord returns to earth in glory (Matt. 25:31). The context indicates that Peter is talking about the glorious return of the Lord (1 Pet. 4:5, 7).

Rejoice with exultation. For the persecuted believer, there is joy now and more joy to come when the Lord returns. Heaven honors those who shine for Jesus (Matt. 5:12).

4:14 **Reviled for the name of Christ**. If you are insulted, mocked, or slandered for being a Christian.

You are blessed; see 1 Pet. 3:14.

The Spirit of glory and of God is the Holy Spirit, who both rests on you and dwells in you (Rom. 8:9). The Holy Spirit doesn't come and go, but he abides in you forever (John 14:17).

Rests on you. When you are reviled for the sake of Christ, it means that those in darkness can see the touch of God on your life. They may call you a troublemaker and throw you into prison, but their slander is evidence that the Lord is with you and on you.

---

1 Peter 4:15–16

15 Make sure that none of you suffers as a murderer, or thief, or
evildoer, or a troublesome meddler; 16 but if anyone suffers as a
Christian, he is not to be ashamed, but is to glorify God in this name.

4:15 **Suffers**. There's good suffering and bad suffering. If you are persecuted for being a Christian, that's a reason to rejoice (1

Pet. 4:13–14). But if you are locked up for being a criminal, you have nothing to be proud of.

4:16 **Suffers as a Christian**. Christians may suffer trials on account of their faith in Christ (1 Pet. 1:6). Whether you are slandered as an evildoer (1 Pet. 2:12, 3:16), or experience a fiery ordeal (1 Pet. 4:12), learn to see these trials as an opportunity to bring glory to God.

Christian. This word, which appears only three times in the Bible, means a follower of Christ (Acts 11:26, 26:28). In a New Testament context, it does not mean a follower of a religion called Christianity. Josephus, in his *Antiquities*, recorded that Christ rose on the third day and the tribe of Christians were "so named from him."

Not to be ashamed. Hold your head high, for you are a dearly-loved child of God.

The devil wants to shipwreck your faith and undermine your good conscience. He will tell you lies to make you feel like you've done something wrong, or that your faith isn't real. But we should never be ashamed for being recognized as a follower of Christ. Indeed, we should count it as a blessing (1 Pet. 4:14).

Glorify God. Thank God that you have been counted worthy of the name Christian.

In this name. In the early days of the church, the label Christian was considered derogatory, but there is no shame in being recognized as a follower of Christ.

---

1 Peter 4:17–19

17 For it is time for judgment to begin with the household of God;
and if it begins with us first, what will be the outcome for those who
do not obey the gospel of God? 18 And "If it is with difficulty that the
righteous is saved, what will become of the godless man and the
sinner?" 19 Therefore, those also who suffer according to the will of
God shall entrust their souls to a faithful Creator in doing what is
right.

4:17 **It is time for judgment to begin**. The church was about to face a period of increased persecution.

The scattered believers had already experienced a measure of suffering (1 Pet. 2:19–20), but now the judgment, or condemnation, of Christians had become a fiery ordeal (1 Pet. 4:12). The apostle Paul was dead, and in a year or two Peter himself would be crucified (2 Pet. 1:14). If you were a follower of Christ, martyrdom was a real prospect (Rev. 2:10).

In the beginning, the New Testament church only had to deal with persecution from the religious Jews. But now the Gentiles (e.g., the idol-worshippers and imperious Romans), who formerly had been agnostic about the gospel and the rise of the church, had come to an unfavorable judgment. Along with the Jews, they began to condemn and persecute the church throughout the Roman world (e.g., Heb. 10:32–34, 1 Pet. 2:12).

The household of God. In the New Testament, believers are collectively referred to as the family, or household, of God (Eph. 2:19, 1 Tim. 3:15, 1 Pet. 2:5).

What will be the outcome for those who do not obey the gospel of God? Those who reject the grace of God that is revealed in the gospel will ultimately be destroyed (2 Pet. 3:7). Peter is not saying that we have to go through difficulties to prove ourselves righteous any more than he is saying God disciplines his church with punishment. He's saying choices have consequences. Better to suffer and be reviled for being a Christian than to be lost eternally.

The gospel revealed in the Bible goes by several names. There is the gospel of Jesus Christ (Mark 1:1) or just the gospel of Christ (Rom. 15:19, 1 Cor. 9:12, 2 Cor. 2:12, 9:13, 10:14, Gal. 1:7, Php. 1:27, 1 Th. 3:2). There is the gospel of God (Mark 1:14, Rom 1:1, 15:16, 2 Cor. 11:7, 1 Th. 2:2, 8, 9), the gospel of the blessed God (1 Tim. 1:11), and the gospel of his Son (Rom 1:9). There is the gospel of the kingdom (Matt. 4:23, 9:35, 24:14, Luke 16:16), and the gospel of the glory of Christ (2 Cor. 4:4). These are different labels for the one and only gospel of the grace of God (Acts 20:24).

4:18 **If it is with difficulty**. Being a Christian is no picnic when you are being slandered or persecuted for your faith. Yet it is better to suffer briefly than be lost forever. (The quote is from Proverbs 11:31 as it appears in the Septuagint, the Greek Old Testament.)

The righteous are those who have been made right with God by receiving, through faith, the free gift of Christ's righteousness.

What will become of the godless? They will reap death and destruction (2 Pet. 3:7).

Godless. The original word (*asebes*) is translated elsewhere as ungodly. To be ungodly is to have nothing but contempt for the things of God.

4:19 **Those who suffer according to the will of God**. Those who are persecuted for being Christians. It is not God's will for you to be mistreated, but persecution happens (2 Tim. 3:12).

The wrong way to read this verse (and 1 Pet. 3:17) is, "Sometimes it is God's will for you to suffer." That is not what Peter is saying. The context is persecution (1 Pet. 4:13–14). "If anyone suffers as a Christian" (1 Pet. 4:16). Why would God want you to be persecuted for trusting in him? To "suffer according to the will of God" is to be persecuted because you are in the will of God.

The will of God is for you to put your faith in Jesus and walk in newness of life (1 Pet. 4:2).

A faithful Creator. You can trust the Creator with your life because he is faithful. He will never leave you, never let you down, and never disappoint you. His promises are unbreakable and his love never fails.

Doing what is right. Right believing leads to right living. When your heart is settled in the faithfulness of God, you will live righteously without any conscious effort. The Righteous One will fill your heart with his righteous desires and he will bear his righteous fruit in your life.

---

1 Peter 5

1 Peter 5:1–4

1 Therefore, I exhort the elders among you, as your fellow elder and
witness of the sufferings of Christ, and a partaker also of the glory
that is to be revealed, 2 shepherd the flock of God among you, exercising oversight not under compulsion, but voluntarily, according to
the will of God; and not for sordid gain, but with eagerness; 3 nor yet
as lording it over those allotted to your charge, but proving to be
examples to the flock. 4 And when the Chief Shepherd appears, you
will receive the unfading crown of glory.

5:1 **The elders**. An elder or overseer watches over and cares for the church, a role they fulfil by teaching, praying, and setting a good example (Tit. 1:9, 1 Pet. 5:3, Jas. 5:14).

The elders among you. Although Peter's letter was addressed to scattered believers who had fled Judea and resettled in Asia Minor, it was circulated among churches led by elders. The elders received the letter and read it out in the church.

Your fellow elder. Peter was one of the greatest apostles and a close personal friend of Jesus, yet when writing to churches led by elders, he identified himself as a fellow elder. In doing this he modelled Christlike leadership, which is characterized by humility and setting an example for others to follow.

Witness. Peter reminds us that he was present at the key events of Christ's life and ministry including the crucifixion. In contrast with false teachers who belittle things they haven't experienced and who boast about things they don't understand, Peter had massive credibility.

A partaker also of the glory. Peter was present on the Mount of Transfiguration when the Lord Jesus Christ was unveiled in power and glory (2 Peter 1:16).

The glory that is to be revealed is synonymous with the salvation that is to be revealed when Jesus Christ returns and we are clothed with glory (1 Pet. 1:5). Peter is saying, "On the mountain I had a taste of what is coming when the Lord returns in glory."

5:2 **Shepherd the flock**. An elder is not a CEO or general but a shepherd like Jesus (1 Pet. 2:25). The original word for shepherd (*poimaino*) is related to a noun (*poimen*) that is sometimes translated as pastor (Eph. 4:11). A pastor is a shepherd. The exhortation to care for the sheep is something Peter heard from the Good Shepherd himself (John 21:15–17).

Exercising oversight. Shepherds watch over and care for the sheep.

Voluntarily. Willingly.

Not for sordid gain. Don't become a pastor for the money. Do it because it is a privilege and an honor to care for the Shepherd's sheep.

5:3 **Lording**. As Jesus taught and modelled, Christlike leaders are to be servant-hearted and not lord it over others (Matt. 20:25–26). Sadly, his words and example are forgotten in cultures characterized by control and coercion. When church leaders are put on pedestals, the opportunity for abuse is never far away.

Examples. A godly pastor does not throw their weight around like a tyrant but sets an example for others to follow. They have the same mindset as Paul, who said, "Imitate me, as I imitate Christ" (1 Cor. 11:1).

What does a pastor do? Pastors are asked to do a hundred different things, but in the Bible they mainly do three things: they set an example for others to follow, they prayerfully watch over those in their care, and they teach so that the body of Christ may be strengthened and equipped (See Acts 20:28, Eph. 4:11, Tit. 1:9, Heb. 13:17, 1 Pet. 5:2–3). Not all teachers are pastors, but all pastors are teachers, in one form or another.

5:4 **The Chief Shepherd**. Although pastors are shepherds, the sheep belong to the Chief Shepherd, Jesus Christ (1 Pet. 2:25).

The unfading crown of glory is synonymous with the crown of life that Jesus gives to all who love him (Jas. 1:12). Crowns are given to all the children of the King, and the least crown, if there is such a thing, is more glorious than the most splendid crown on earth.

1 Peter 5:5–7

5 You younger men, likewise, be subject to your elders; and all of
you, clothe yourselves with humility toward one another, for "God
is opposed to the proud, but gives grace to the humble." 6 Therefore
humble yourselves under the mighty hand of God, that he may exalt
you at the proper time, 7 casting all your anxiety on him, because he
cares for you.

5:5 **Younger men**. Since the original words are gender neutral, this should be read as younger *people*.

Be subject means to yield or submit. It is something the young people do for their elders and not something those who are older impose on those who are younger. It's an act of love from the one submitting, not an act of control imposed by the one being submitted to (1 Pet. 2:13).

Elders; see 1 Pet. 5:1.

All of you. The original word for subject (*hupotasso*) appears twice in this verse, first in connection with younger men, then in connection with everyone else. As other translations have it: "All of you be subject one to another." As in all matters of love, submission is a two-way street.

Humility is the defining characteristic of any Christian relationship or organization. Humility attracts the grace of God.

God is opposed to the proud. The proud who resist grace will find God resisting them. (The quote is from Proverbs 3:34 as it appears in the Septuagint, the Greek Old Testament.)

One way that God resists the proud is by applying the hammer of the law to the hard and stubborn heart. To those who say, "I have no need of grace for I am good enough," the law replies, "You are not good at all. You are a lawbreaker, deserving of death, and in desperate need of grace."

Grace captures the goodwill, lovingkindness, and favor of God that is freely given to us so that we may partake in his divine life. Grace is God's divine aid that supernaturally empowers you to be who he made you to be.

But gives grace to the humble. Without humility there can be no repentance, and without repentance there can be no turning to God and no salvation. We all need grace, but grace only comes to those who are honest enough to acknowledge their need for it (Jas. 4:6).

5:6 **Humble yourselves**. As an act of love, we give preference to one another (Rom. 12:10). Note that we don't humble others; we humble ourselves.

The mighty hand of God. When we submit to spouses, bosses, and one another in love (1 Pet. 2:18, 3:8, 5:5), we are submitting to the Lord of all. This is particularly true if the person we are submitting to is unreasonable. In the natural, they may not deserve our love. But we love them anyway and we pray for them because God loves them and his love burns in our hearts.

He may exalt you at the proper time. True promotion comes from the Lord and it comes in his good timing.

5:7 **Casting**. God wants you to live carefree and untroubled by worry. To cast your cares is to say, "Take these burdens, Lord, for I will carry them no longer." Since you belong to the Lord (1 Pet. 2:9), your burdens belong to him. They are not yours but his and he is well able to bear them.

He cares for you. God is not a distant deity but your loving Father who is interested in everything about you (see Luke 12:7). You are the apple of his eye.

---

1 Peter 5:8–9

[8] Be of sober spirit, be on the alert. Your adversary, the devil, prowls around like a roaring lion, seeking someone to devour. [9] But resist him, firm in your faith, knowing that the same experiences of suffering are being accomplished by your brethren who are in the world.

5:8 **Sober spirit**. Be clearheaded and live with your eyes open.

Be on the alert. Don't get caught napping. Watch your thought life and guard your heart. Take care not to heed any message that might distract you from simple faith in Jesus.

Adversary. The original word (*antidikos*) means an opponent in a lawsuit. The devil is a legalist who will try to bring charges against you. He will accuse you of being a failure, being neglectful, being imperfect. He does this to undermine your faith and provoke you to respond in your own strength. A better response is to take those charges and accusations and give them to Jesus your Advocate who defends you (1 John 2:1).

The devil is a defeated and disarmed enemy (Heb. 2:14). The only way he can defeat you is by deceiving you and filling you with fear and anxiety. He will tell you that God is angry with you or that you are beyond the reach of his grace. "You have committed the unforgivable sin and God won't accept you." Ignore his lies; listen to Jesus. Read the previous verse and cast all your anxiety on the Lord who cares for you.

Like a roaring lion seeking. What sort of lion roars while it seeks its prey? This toothless lion is all roar and no bite. He's trying to frighten you with his lies and accusations because that's his only trick.

Seeking someone. The devil can't just devour people; he can only go after those who have wandered from the Good Shepherd and aren't standing firm in the faith (see next verse).

5:9 **Resist him**. We actively resist the devil by submitting to God (Jas. 4:7).

Spiritual warfare for the Christian is less about shouting at the devil and more about believing that Jesus is Lord over whatever situation we face (1 Cor. 15:57). Unbelief says we must engage the enemy and fight for the victory, but faith declares that Jesus has already won. Unbelief cowers before the name of the adversary, whether it's disease, debt, or depression, but faith exalts the Name that is above every name.

Firm in your faith. To be firm in the faith we must stand firm in the grace of God (1 Pet. 5:12).

Suffering for being a Christian (see 1 Pet. 4:16).

Your brethren. Fellow believers around the world. When we go through trials it's tempting to think that we are alone and nobody understands what we are going through. That is rarely the case.

---

1 Peter 5:10–11

10 After you have suffered for a little while, the God of all grace, who
called you to his eternal glory in Christ, will himself perfect, confirm,
strengthen and establish you. 11 To him be dominion forever and
ever. Amen.

5:10 **A little while**. All earthly afflictions are temporary and fleeting in comparison with eternity (2 Cor. 4:17).

The God of all grace. All love and grace originates with God. Grace is what the unconditional love of God looks like from our side. Grace is love come down.

Manmade religion portrays God as an angry deity who can be bought off with sacrifices and good works. But the God that Jesus revealed sits on a throne of grace (Heb. 4:16). He blesses us for no other reason than he loves us.

Who called you; see 1 Peter 1:15.

Glory; see 1 Pet. 1:21.

Will himself perfect, confirm, strengthen and establish you. We are saved and kept by grace.

Most Christians know that it is on account of God's grace that we are saved (Acts 15:11, Eph. 2:8, 2 Tim. 1:9), forgiven (Eph. 1:7), justified (Rom. 3:24, Tit. 3:7) and made alive with Christ (Eph. 2:5). But they may not appreciate that *all* of God's blessings come by grace (Eph. 1:3).

Grace builds us up (Acts 20:32), empowers us to do good works (Gal. 2:9), makes us fruitful (Col. 1:6), and prospers us (2 Cor. 8:9, 9:8). Grace gives us hope (2 Th. 2:6) and enables us to reign in life (Rom. 5:21). Grace is not merely for "sinners" and those outside the kingdom. Grace is for all of us, every day.

Perfect. The original verb (*katartizo*) means to repair, adjust, equip, and thoroughly complete. Dead religion says you have to fix yourself, but the gospel of grace says you can trust the Lord to complete the good work he has begun in you (Php. 1:6).

Confirm. The original verb (*sterizo*) means to fix or set firmly in place. It is usually translated as establish and strengthen, so Peter is repeating himself for emphasis.

5:11 **Dominion**. Peter repeats part of his praise prayer of 1 Peter 4:11.

---

1 Peter 5:12–14

12 Through Silvanus, our faithful brother (for so I regard him), I have
written to you briefly, exhorting and testifying that this is the true
grace of God. Stand firm in it! 13 She who is in Babylon, chosen
together with you, sends you greetings, and so does my son, Mark.
14 Greet one another with a kiss of love. Peace be to you all who are
in Christ.

5:12 **Silvanus** was the Romanized name of Silas, a colleague of both Peter and Paul. Silvanus delivered Peter's letter to the churches in the five Roman provinces of Asia Minor (1 Pet. 1:1). Silvanus would have been known to these churches as he had passed through the region on his travels with Paul.

The true grace of God can be contrasted with the counterfeit grace preached by false teachers. False grace promotes sin and self-trust while true grace inspires you to rely on Christ Jesus. Sadly, there have always been some who preach a false kind of grace, and Peter will have more to say about them in the second chapter of his second letter.

Stand firm in it! Everything in the Christian life depends upon us standing firm in the true grace of God. Since God's grace comes to us through his Son (John 1:17), Peter is saying, "Hold fast to Jesus and let nothing move you."

5:13 **She who is in Babylon**. Who is she? Nobody knows. She could be a woman (Peter's wife? John Mark's mother?) or the church itself.

Babylon was probably a code name for Rome. Peter sent his letter from Rome to believers in nearby provinces (1 Pet. 1:1).

Mark is widely believed to be John Mark, the probable author of the Gospel of Mark. John Mark was friends with both Paul and Peter (Acts 12:25). Just as Paul called Timothy a spiritual son in the faith (1 Tim. 1:18), Peter considered Mark to be a spiritual son. Papias, the Bishop of Hierapolis, considered Mark's Gospel to be based on Peter's memories.

5:14 **A kiss of love**. Like the Jews before them (Gen. 27:26, Luke 7:45), the early Christians greeted one another with a kiss of friendship (Acts 20:37). Paul called this greeting a holy kiss (1 Cor. 16:20, 2 Cor. 13:12, 1 Thess. 5:26). Peter called it a kiss of love.

All who are in Christ. Believers. You are in Christ and he is in you. There are no stages to spiritual union with Christ; you are either in Christ or you need to be.

2 Peter 1

2 Peter 1:1–2

1 Simon Peter, a bond-servant and apostle of Jesus Christ, to those
who have received a faith of the same kind as ours, by the righteousness of our God and Savior, Jesus Christ: 2 Grace and peace be
multiplied to you in the knowledge of God and of Jesus our Lord;

1:1 **Simon Peter**; see 1 Pet. 1:1.

A bond-servant or bondslave; see 1 Pet. 2:16.

An apostle; see 1 Pet. 1:1.

Received a faith. Faith is not something to manufacture, but something to receive. It is a gift from God (Eph. 2:8). Faith comes from hearing about the love of God that has been revealed to us through Jesus Christ (Rom. 10:17).

A faith of the same kind as ours. There are different kinds of faith: There's dead faith and saving faith (Jas. 2:14). There's faith in ourselves, and faith in Christ. There's faith that leads to works of self-righteousness, and faith that receives the gift of Christ's righteousness. If you have the latter kind of faith, you have the same kind of faith as Peter and the apostles.

You may worry that you have insufficient faith or the wrong sort of faith. But if you believe that God has made you righteous for no reason other than he loves you, then you have the same precious faith as the apostles. Or perhaps you worry that you have insufficient faith or that you might have a failure of faith and deny Jesus. Something like this happened to Peter, yet he did not fall because Jesus was praying for him (Luke 22:32). You are not kept safe by your faithfulness to Christ but by his faithfulness to you. Christ lives in you, and it is his faith and his faithfulness that sustains you (Gal. 2:20).

The righteousness of our God. God demonstrates his justice and rightness by freely giving us the faith we need. God asks nothing of us except that we trust him, and then he gives us the faith to trust him. How gracious, how good, and how righteous is our God!

God and Savior, Jesus Christ. Jesus is both Savior and God, meaning the Son is equal with the Father. "I and the Father are one" (John 10:30).

1:2 **Grace and peace**. Peter was familiar with Paul's letters (2 Pet. 3:16) and seems to have adopted Paul's traditional greeting (see Rom. 1:7). Grace encompasses all the blessings of God (Eph. 1:3), and peace is the fruit of receiving his great grace. Someone who is relying on their works instead of resting in his grace will have little peace because there is always more work to be done.

Multiplied. The original word (*plethuno*) is the same word that is translated as fullest measure in 1 Peter 1:2. God's grace multiplies and abounds as we grow in our understanding of his Son and what he has done for us (2 Pet. 3:18).

Knowledge. Every spiritual blessing comes to us through our knowledge of the Lord – who he is, what he has done for us, what he has said and is now saying. We are not blessed on account of our effort or performance; we are blessed as we grow in the grace and knowledge of Jesus Christ (2 Pet. 3:18).

Jesus our Lord. The original word for Lord (*kyrios*) means the One who is supreme above all. Some called Jesus rabbi, prophet, or the Nazarene, but believers call him Lord (Rom. 10:13).

---

2 Peter 1:3–4

[3] seeing that his divine power has granted to us everything pertaining
to life and godliness, through the true knowledge of him who called
us by his own glory and excellence. [4] For by these he has granted to
us his precious and magnificent promises, so that by them you may
become partakers of the divine nature, having escaped the corrupt-
tion that is in the world by lust.

1:3 **His divine power**. Manmade religion is fuelled by blood, sweat, and tears, but the gospel of grace rests on God's supernatural provision and power. Religion demands that you do more and work harder, but grace declares, "See what God has done and receive!"

Everything you need for today, tomorrow, and forevermore has been provided freely by grace and comes to you through your knowledge of Jesus Christ. Whatever questions you may be asking and whatever problems you may be facing, your answer begins with a deeper revelation of the Lord and his fathomless love for you.

Life. God has given you everything you need for a good and healthy life. You have no needs that are not amply supplied by your heavenly Father (Ps. 23:1, Php. 4:19).

The true knowledge of him can be contrasted with the false words of false teachers (2 Pet 2:1, 3).

Religion and philosophy will fill your mind with all kinds of head knowledge, but true growth comes via spiritual revelation. You do not need to know the Bible cover to cover to walk in the power and provision of God; you just need to know Christ in your situation. In him are hidden all the treasures of wisdom and knowledge (Col. 2:3). All the blessings of heaven are ours through him (Eph. 1:3).

Him who called us. God calls us to himself so that we might be saved; see 1 Peter 1:15.

Glory. The original noun (*doxa*) means majesty, magnificence, splendor, preeminence, and exalted.

Excellence; see 2 Pet. 1:5.

1:4 **Promises**. The precious promises of God are invitations to the abundant life that is ours in Christ. Just as Joshua led the Israelites into the Promised Land, Jesus has brought you into the Land of Promises, and it is a good land flowing with milk and honey. Whatever situation you are facing, God has a precious promise for you to stand on.

Partakers of the divine nature. Christian, you are one with the Lord. You share the nature and mind of Christ (1 Cor. 2:16). "You may become partakers" means you can participate in Christ's divine life here and now. However, you will not experience this blessed life if you are heeding the lies of DIY religion. This is why Peter opens his letter by reminding us of God's gracious provision – "his divine power has granted us everything" – before warning us, in the next chapter, to steer clear of false teachers.

Escaped the corruption. The broken and corrupt person you used to be died with Christ and no longer lives (Gal. 2:20). You have a choice. You can walk according to the old and cursed ways of the flesh, or you can participate in the new and blessed life of Christ Jesus (1 Pet. 1:14–15).

Lust. The selfish desires of the flesh that corrupt us.

---

2 Peter 1:5–7

[5] Now for this very reason also, applying all diligence, in your faith
supply moral excellence, and in your moral excellence, knowledge,
[6] and in your knowledge, self-control, and in your self-control, perseverance, and in your perseverance, godliness, [7] and in your godliness, brotherly kindness, and in your brotherly kindness, love.

1:5 **For this very reason**. Take advantage of God's promises so that you may participate in his divine life. God's promises are true whether you believe them or not, but they won't do you any good unless you believe them.

Diligence. The original noun (*spoude*) can be translated as speed or haste. It does not mean work hard for years and years. Peter is saying, "Don't waste time walking after the flesh and the desires of your old way of life, but be eager and earnest to put God's promises to work."

Faith is the foundation for all Christian growth, but we do not provide the faith that makes us grow. Faith is a gift to receive, and we get it by hearing the good news of Jesus Christ. As we allow the Holy Spirit to reveal more of God's love to us – love that has been revealed to us through his Son – our trust in him grows and our faith is strengthened (2 Pet. 3:18).

Supply. Jesus is your rich supply (Col. 2:19). The wrong way to read this list is to think that we must manufacture or supply our own faith, excellence, self-control, etc. In the economy of grace, everything we need is abundantly supplied by God (2 Pet. 1:11). Whatever needs we have the Lord will supply (Php. 4:19).

Excellence. By the grace of God, you will do well in life. Because God's grace is powerful, you can expect to excel with your God-given gifts. (The original word (*arete*) simply means excellence. The adjective *moral* has been added by translators.) History is littered with examples of godly men and women who excelled in the fields of art, science, politics, business, and education.

Knowledge. Because you have the mind of Christ (1 Cor. 2:16), you can know the will of God for your life. As you lean on the Holy Spirit, you can discover heavenly solutions for earthly problems.

1:6 **Self-control** or discipline is a fruit of the spirit (Gal. 5:22–23) and your antidote to the lusts of the flesh. Self-control is not about saying no to sin but saying yes to Jesus.

Perseverance or endurance. Your God-given faith gives you the strength to persevere and endure (Jas. 1:3). Because Christ endured, you will endure.

Godliness or holy conduct. You don't become holy by acting holy. But since you are the holy child of a holy Father, you can be holy in all your conduct; see 1 Pet. 1:15.

1:7 **Brotherly kindness** or affection for those in the family of God. The followers of Cain attack and kill their brothers (1 John 3:12), but the followers of Christ are known for their brotherly love (John 13:35). We love one another by clothing ourselves with humility, being hospitable, and pursuing harmony (1 Pet. 3:8, 4:9, 5:5).

Love is the ultimate expression of healed humanity (1 Tim. 1:5). God is love, and when we abide in his love, we are empowered to love others (1 John 4:19).

2 Peter 1:8–9

[8] For if these qualities are yours and are increasing, they render you neither useless nor unfruitful in the true knowledge of our Lord Jesus Christ. [9] For he who lacks these qualities is blind or short-sighted, having forgotten his purification from his former sins.

1:8 **These qualities** are the seven traits of the Christian life just listed: excellence, knowledge, self-control, perseverance, godliness, brotherly kindness, and love (2 Pet. 1:5–7). These qualities describe the good life that is ours in Christ. To experience this new life – to partake of his divine nature – you need to grow in the grace and knowledge of Jesus Christ (2 Pet. 3:18).

Unfruitful. When we abide in the Vine, we bear his fruit effortlessly. But when we walk in the flesh – we lean on our own resources and understanding – we become ineffective and unfruitful. Peter provides an example of how this can happen in the next verse.

True knowledge; see 2 Pet. 1:3.

1:9 **Blind or short-sighted**. Because spiritual growth comes from revelation, the one thing that stops us from maturing is spiritual blindness. If we fail to see that our old self and our old sins were dealt with once and for all on the cross, we will not grow. The remedy to this sort of blindness is to open our eyes to the realities of our new life in Christ.

Having forgotten. Forgetting that we are forgiven renders us unfruitful.

The gospel of grace declares you are eternally and completely forgiven (Acts 13:38, Eph. 1:7, Col. 2:13, 1 John 2:12). You have been cleansed from all sin (1 John 1:7). But if you forget you are forgiven, you'll be susceptible to the lie that says there are things you must do to get forgiven.

Purification. You have been cleansed from all sin (1 John 1:7). All your sins – past, present, and future – were carried away by the Lamb of God (John 1:29, 1 John 2:2).

Receiving and walking in God's forgiveness is where the rubber of your faith hits the road of his grace. If you wish to grow in grace, you need to believe that your old sins are gone. In Christ you are righteous, holy, and as pure as the driven snow (Is. 1:18).

Former sins. Sinning was a part of your old life, and it has no place in the new life you share with Christ (1 John 3:9). This is not to suggest you will never sin, but you are a sinner no more. You are a royal priest and a citizen of a holy nation (1 Pet. 2:9).

---

2 Peter 1:10–11

10 Therefore, brethren, be all the more diligent to make certain about
his calling and choosing you; for as long as you practice these things,
you will never stumble; 11 for in this way the entrance into the eternal
kingdom of our Lord and Savior Jesus Christ will be abundantly supplied to you.

1:10 **Diligent**. The original verb (*spoudazo*) can be translated as hasten, be earnest, or hurry. "Make this a priority."

Make certain about his calling. Don't be in two minds about the certainty of God's hold on your life (John 10:28). He who called you and chose you will perfect, confirm, strengthen, and establish you (1 Pet. 5:10).

Believers stumble into dead works when they are unsure about their position in Christ. They forget they are forgiven or they think they need to complete what Christ began. "Jesus got me started, but the rest is up to me." But whenever we look to ourselves to supply that which God has supplied, we fall from grace. For this reason we need to be diligent to establish our hearts in the certainty of our Father's love. We need to allow the Holy Spirit to convince us that we are holy and righteous and one with the Lord. We need to abandon our old ways of thinking and learn to walk in the new way of the Spirit.

His calling and choosing. God called you and God chose you (Eph. 1:18, 1 Pet. 1:1, 15). Your salvation is not something to be dismissed as a mere invention or a fleeting spiritual experience. The Maker of heaven and earth called you and you responded in faith. The day you were born again was the single most important day of your life.

Practice these things. Make it a habit of looking to the Lord for your supply.

You will never stumble. When your eyes are fixed on Jesus, you'll never put a foot wrong.

1:11 **The entrance into the eternal kingdom**. You will have a rich assurance of your salvation.

Just as we can be certain of God's call (see previous verse), we can be certain of our salvation or entrance into the eternal kingdom. Yet many Christians are uncertain. They wonder if they are forgiven (verse 9) or if God really called them (verse 10). The remedy to this sort of anxiety is to remind ourselves of the Truth who lives within us (next verse).

Abundantly supplied. The same God who supplies you with faith (2 Pet. 1:1), precious promises (2 Pet. 1:4), and everything else you need for life and godliness (2 Pet. 1:3), has abundantly provided you with an entrance into his kingdom. He did not sneak you in through the side door. He adopted you into his family, clothed you with the garments of salvation, and wrapped you in the robe of his righteousness (Is. 61:10). Truly, you are saved by grace (Eph. 2:8).

---

2 Peter 1:12–15

[12] Therefore, I will always be ready to remind you of these things,
even though you already know them, and have been established in
the truth which is present with you. [13] I consider it right, as long as I
am in this earthly dwelling, to stir you up by way of reminder,
[14] knowing that the laying aside of my earthly dwelling is imminent,
as also our Lord Jesus Christ has made clear to me. [15] And I will also
be diligent that at any time after my departure you will be able to call
these things to mind.

1:12 **Remind you**. Even people who have been in church for years need to be reminded of God's gracious provision.

You already know that you have been forgiven, but you might forget (2 Pet. 1:9). You already know that God loves you, is pleased with you, and thinks the world of you, but you might get distracted and start to drift. We all need reminders lest we wander from the truth.

Present with you. Jesus is the Truth who dwells within the believer and empowers us to live in the new way of the spirit.

1:13 **This earthly dwelling** is your physical body, which can be contrasted with your inner self (your spirit and soul) or hidden person (1 Pet. 3:4). Peter is saying, "For as long as I'm on this earth, I'm going to remind you of God's abundant supply."

Stir you up. Rouse or wake you up.

Reminder; see previous verse.

1:14 **Laying aside**. For the believer, death is little more than putting off this mortal body (or earthly dwelling).

Imminent. Peter believed that he was going to die soon. Jesus told Peter how he would spend the final years of his life (John 21:18–19). Apparently the prophecy was being fulfilled at the time of this letter, which was possibly written from a Roman prison. Early Church tradition teaches that Peter was beheaded by Nero in Rome in AD64.

1:15 **Diligent**. Peter wrote letters to ensure that we wouldn't forget what he said.

My departure. My death.

Call these things to mind. We need to remember what we have been taught (see 2 Pet. 1:12).

---

2 Peter 1:16–18

[16] For we did not follow cleverly devised tales when we made known to you the power and coming of our Lord Jesus Christ, but we were eyewitnesses of his majesty. [17] For when he received honor and glory from God the Father, such an utterance as this was made to him by the Majestic Glory, "This is my beloved Son with whom I am well-

pleased"— [18] and we ourselves heard this utterance made from heaven when we were with him on the holy mountain.

1:16 **Tales**. Myths. Peter may be alluding to Gnostic speculations or Jewish myths (Tit. 1:14).

We made known to you. "We told you that we saw our Lord Jesus Christ unveiled in power and glory." Since it is unlikely that Peter visited the regions to which this letter was sent, he is likely referring to something he said in his first letter (e.g., 1 Pet. 5:1).

The power and coming. Jesus came to earth as a humble baby, but he will return as a triumphant King.

Eyewitnesses. Peter reminds us that his testimony is based on first-hand experience.

To the modern believer, Peter stands as a giant in the church. But in the early days there may have been some who dismissed him. "Isn't he a Galilean fisherman?" "Didn't he deny Jesus three times?" Whatever his flaws may have been, no one can deny that Peter had a front-row seat to the life and ministry of Jesus Christ. In contrast with false teachers speaking false words (2 Pet. 2:1, 3), Peter speaks the truth.

Eyewitnesses of his majesty. On the Mount of Transfiguration, Peter, James and John glimpsed the Lord in all his kingly glory (Matt. 17:2).

1:17 **He received honor and glory**. On the Mount of Transfiguration the Son of God was honored by God himself, leaving the disciples in no doubt as to Christ's true identity.

Glory; see 2 Pet. 1:3.

This is my beloved Son. God the Father loves God the Son. The heavenly affirmation was heard by all at Christ's baptism (Matt. 3:17) and was repeated on the mountain (Matt. 17:5).

1:18 **Heard**. "We heard God speak on the mountain." Again, Peter presents himself as a credible witness. In contrast with false teachers who speak of things they don't know or understand (2 Pet. 2:18), Peter heard the audible voice of God.

The holy mountain. The Mount of Transfiguration.

2 Peter 1:19–21

[19] So we have the prophetic word made more sure, to which you do well to pay attention as to a lamp shining in a dark place, until the day dawns and the morning star arises in your hearts. [20] But know this first of all, that no prophecy of Scripture is a matter of one's own interpretation, [21] for no prophecy was ever made by an act of human will, but men moved by the Holy Spirit spoke from God.

1:19 **The prophetic word**. Old Testament prophecies concerning the Messiah (e.g., Is. 9:6–7, 22:22, 53:3–9, 61:1–2).

Made more sure. The audible voice of God (on the mountain) confirmed the written word of God (recorded by the prophets). We can be sure that nothing God says to us will contradict what he has revealed in the scriptures. Peter heard God speaking on the mountain, and what he heard confirmed what he knew from the old prophecies: Jesus was no mere rabbi or prophet. He is the Son of God and the King of kings.

Pay attention to what the prophets said. Knowing what God has said through the scriptures is how we protect ourselves from false teachers who deny the Lord (2 Pet. 2:1) and mockers who say he will never return (2 Pet. 3:3–4).

A lamp. The word of God shines in a dark world and by its light we find the true path (Ps. 119:105).

The day dawns. The day the Lord returns in glory. For now, we navigate a dark world by the light of God's sure word. But one day the Son will come like the rising sun, and all darkness will go.

The morning star is Jesus himself (Rev. 22:16). We already have his Spirit within us, but when he returns to earth, we will have him in person (Rev. 2:28). When that day dawns and the morning star rises in our hearts, all things will be made new (2 Pet. 3:13). There will be no more sorrow and no more death. When Christ returns, it will be the beginning of life such as we can only dream of.

1:20 **Interpretation**. The prophecies in the Bible weren't invented by people but were divinely inspired.

1:21 **Moved by the Holy Spirit**. The Holy Spirit revealed the words of God, and the prophets spoke or wrote them down. We can be convinced that all prophecy recorded in Scripture is from God.

The Holy Spirit or the Spirit of Christ (1 Pet. 1:11) or the Spirit of glory (1 Pet. 4:14) gave the prophets spiritual revelation.

2 Peter 2

2 Peter 2:1

1 But false prophets also arose among the people, just as there will also be false teachers among you, who will secretly introduce destructive heresies, even denying the Master who bought them, bringing swift destruction upon themselves.

2:1 **But false prophets**. The counterfeit follows the authentic. In the Old Testament, the Israelites were blessed by true prophets and troubled by false prophets such as Balaam (2 Pet. 2:15).

False teachers among you. Just as there were false prophets among the children of Israel, there are false teachers who infiltrate the church. Like Jesus (Matt. 7:15), Paul (2 Cor. 11:13), John (1 John 4:1), and Jude (Jude 1:4), Peter felt a strong need to warn believers about these dangerous people and their destructive teachings.

Secretly. These wolves in sheep's clothing are sneaky. They use spiritual jargon to disguise their real agenda, which is to feed their greed (2 Pet. 2:3).

Destructive heresies. False teachers usually come in two stripes: some preach law (Acts 15:5), while others preach license (Jude 1:4, Rev. 2:15). These false teachers were in the latter camp. They taught that grace is a license to sin (see next verse).

Licentious teachings are destructive because they undermine your faith and seduce the vulnerable (2 Pet. 2:14). Left unchecked, false teachers can wreck families and split churches.

Denying the Master. These false teachers were not misguided Christians but ungodly people who denied the Lord and were unacquainted with the Holy Spirit (Jude 1:19). How did they deny the Lord? Perhaps they did not believe that Jesus was fully man and fully God (1 John 4:2, 2 John 1:7). Maybe they questioned whether he was the Son of God and the Savior (1 John 2:22, 4:3, 5:10). These teachers embraced the trappings of religion, but they didn't know Jesus and he didn't know them (Matt. 7:23).

It's plain from the context that Peter is talking about false teachers, the sort of people that Jesus and Paul referred to as ravenous or savage wolves (Matt. 7:15, Acts 20:29). Yet some Christians worry that Peter is talking about *them*. "I denied the Lord once." Well, so did Peter (Luke 22:34). Don't confuse apples with oranges. A Christian who stumbles and says something regrettable is acting contrary to their true nature. After Peter denied the Master, he wept bitterly (Luke 22:62). In contrast, a false teacher who is enslaved to corruption and never stops sinning is just doing what comes naturally (2 Pet. 2:14, 19).

Who bought them. Jesus gave himself as a ransom for all (1 Tim. 2:6). With his blood he ransomed all of us, including false teachers. That doesn't mean everyone is saved, but everyone is free to leave the prison of sin because the ransom has been paid. "You have been bought with a price" (1 Cor. 6:20).

Swift destruction. Those who attack God's family put themselves on a fast track to destruction (2 Pet. 3:7). Their time is short and their destruction swift because the Judge is right at the door (Jas. 5:9).

---

2 Peter 2:2–3

2 Many will follow their sensuality, and because of them the way of
the truth will be maligned; 3 and in their greed they will exploit you
with false words; their judgment from long ago is not idle, and their
destruction is not asleep.

2:2 **Sensuality**. The original word (*aselgeia*) means licentiousness or lasciviousness. (This word appears three times in this chapter: 2 Pet. 2:2, 7, 18.) These false teachers can be recognized by their immoral lifestyles.

Jesus died to set us free, but we can lose our freedom through legalism or licentiousness. The former puts price tags on the grace of God, while the latter removes the price tags from sin.

Licentiousness says: do what you will, for we are under grace not law. It's a partial truth (all things are permissible) that leads to captivity and death (not all things are beneficial; see 1 Cor. 6:12).

The way of the truth will be maligned. Licentious teachers are bad advertisements for Jesus, and they make the church look bad. Their fraudulent lifestyles reinforce the perception that the church is full of hypocrites, and they hinder people from coming to the kingdom (see 2 Pet. 2:14).

2:3 **Greed**. Like Balaam the prophet who loved the wages of unrighteousness, these fraudsters are in it for the money (2 Pet. 2:15).

Exploit you. They want your money, your endorsement, and your social media likes and shares. They have no interest in helping you grow in grace. To them you are a resource to be mined.

False words from false teachers amount to a false gospel. While good teachers impart truth that leads to freedom and godliness, false teachers propagate lies that lead to sin and bondage.

Judgment from long ago. Their condemnation has been a long time coming, but it's coming. Those who deny the Lord and attack his bride are heading for trouble (2 Pet. 3:7). In the following verses Peter provides three examples of how God deals with the unrighteous: the angels who rebelled, the ancient world, and the wicked cities of Sodom and Gomorrah.

Their destruction; see 2 Pet. 3:7.

---

2 Peter 2:4–5

4 For if God did not spare angels when they sinned, but cast them into hell and committed them to pits of darkness, reserved for judgment; 5 and did not spare the ancient world, but preserved Noah, a preacher of righteousness, with seven others, when he brought a flood upon the world of the ungodly;

2:4 **Angels**. Presumably these are angels who rebelled against the Lord and fell with Satan (Luke 10:18). But we cannot say for sure as the Bible says almost nothing about them. Peter says the angels were cast down, while Jude says they abandoned their heavenly abode (Jude 1:6).

Hell. The original word (*tartaroo*) is not a noun but a verb that means to incarcerate. It is derived from the Greek word Tartarus, a subterranean place of gloom and darkness. Tartarus is not Hades, the abode of the dead. Neither is it the fiery Hell of which Jesus spoke (Matt. 5:22).

There is some mystery here. Is Peter speaking literally (fallen angels are locked up in some dark pit) or figuratively (fallen angels are unable to be delivered from darkness)? Are fallen angels also known as demons? What we can say is that fallen angels (like demons; Matt. 8:29) are confined in some way until Judgment Day (Jude 1:6).

2:5 **The ancient world**. The antediluvian world that was destroyed in the great flood.

Noah was known as a righteous man (Gen. 6:9) and an heir of the righteousness which is received by faith (Heb. 11:7).

Preacher of righteousness. Noah encouraged his neighbors to get right with God but they didn't listen.

Ungodly. To be ungodly is to have nothing but contempt for the things of God.

Christ died for the ungodly (Rom. 5:6) and God's desire is to justify the ungodly (Rom. 4:5). But those who choose to live independently of God ultimately cut themselves off from the Source of life (2 Pet. 3:7).

A holy God and ungodliness cannot coexist any more than light and dark can coexist. As the light of God's love shines ever brighter, the darkness must flee, and those who prefer the darkness will find themselves with no place to go.

---

2 Peter 2:6–8

6 and if he condemned the cities of Sodom and Gomorrah to destruction by reducing them to ashes, having made them an example
to those who would live ungodly lives thereafter; 7 and if he rescued
righteous Lot, oppressed by the sensual conduct of unprincipled men
8 (for by what he saw and heard that righteous man, while living
among them, felt his righteous soul tormented day after day by their
lawless deeds),

2:6 **Sodom and Gomorrah** were so wicked that their names became synonymous with depravity and violence. They were hellholes full of every kind of misery. The cries of those they oppressed were so great that they drew the attention of the Lord himself (Gen. 18:20–21).

Destruction. The original word (*katastrophe*) means overturn or overthrown. Sodom and Gomorrah were overturned and burned and the result was a catastrophe. A land that had been compared to the garden of the Lord (Gen. 13:10) was reduced to a smoking ash pit.

Ashes. These corrupt cities were destroyed by fire and brimstone that rained down from heaven (Gen. 19:24).

An example. What happened to Sodom and Gomorrah is a picture of what will happen to the ungodly on Judgment Day (Luke 17:29–30, Jude 1:7).

Ungodly; see previous verse.

2:7 **Righteous Lot**. Lot was righteous because he obeyed the call of God and went to Canaan (Gen 12:4–5). The faith that justifies is always a response to the call of God.

Before the cross, no one could be made righteous with Christ's righteousness. The gift of righteousness had not been given and the "one act of righteousness" had not been done (Rom. 5:18). This is why Old Testament saints such as Abraham were *credited* with righteousness on account of their faith in God (Rom. 4:3).

Like his uncle Abraham, Lot was credited or reckoned righteous on account of his faith in God. But in the new covenant, we are *made* righteous with the righteousness that comes from the Righteous One. (Rom. 5:18–19, 2 Cor. 5:21).

Oppressed means vexed or distressed. Lot moved to Sodom because the town was attractive (Gen. 13:10), but he never adopted the corrupt culture of his Sodomite neighbors. He remained an alien in a strange land, much as we are aliens in a fallen world (1 Pet. 2:11).

Unprincipled men. The men of Sodom were exceedingly wicked and depraved (Gen. 13:13).

2:8 **Tormented**. Sodom was not a good place to raise children and Lot hated living there. His righteous soul was tormented day after day. Yet strangely, he never left. Sodom got involved in a war where Lot and his family were taken captive (Gen. 14:11–16). After he was rescued by Abraham, Lot returned to the wicked town. Even as the fire of heaven was about to fall upon the city, he hesitated. He literally had to be dragged from the city by two angels (Gen. 19:16).

Lot was a righteous man who trusted the Lord, but he was not a wise man. At critical moments in his life he walked by sight and relied on his own natural judgment. Despite his foolishness, Lot and his daughters were saved because God rescued them. We are not saved because we are wise or make good life choices; we are saved because our Rescuer is mighty to save, and his grace is greater than our worst decisions (see Rom. 5:20).

Their lawless deeds. The violent crimes committed by the wicked Sodomites.

Sodom was the kind of town where you risked your life every time you stepped outside your door. The men who ran the city were thugs who took what they wanted and destroyed those who got in their way.

2 Peter 2:9–11

9 then the Lord knows how to rescue the godly from temptation, and to keep the unrighteous under punishment for the day of judgment,
10 and especially those who indulge the flesh in its corrupt desires and despise authority. Daring, self-willed, they do not tremble when they revile angelic majesties,
11 whereas angels who are greater in might and power do not bring a reviling judgment against them before the Lord.

2:9 **The Lord knows how to rescue the godly**. In the day of judgment the godly are rescued while the ungodly are destroyed (2 Pet. 3:7).

The godly are those who belong to God. They are believers, also known as the children or household of God (1 Pet. 4:17).

Temptation. The same God who saved Noah and rescued Lot knows how to deliver you from trials and troubles.

The unrighteous are those who have no interest in getting right with God. God draws them with open arms but they turn their backs. He offers them his righteousness but they scorn his gift. Unrighteous is a synonym for ungodly.

Under punishment. Reserved for punishment. The ungodly and the unrighteous are heading for destruction (2 Pet. 3:7).

The day of judgment. Judgment Day is the day when Jesus is revealed from heaven with his mighty angels in flaming fire (2 Th. 1:7). This day is also known as the day of the Lord (2 Pet. 3:10), the day of Christ (Php 1:10), the day of visitation (1 Pet. 2:12), the day of God (2 Pet. 3:12), the day of eternity (2 Pet. 3:18), the day of wrath (Rom. 2:5), the day of judgment (2 Pet. 2:9, 3:7), or simply the day (2 Pet. 1:19).

2:10 **And especially**. If the unrighteous are in trouble, then greedy fraudsters who malign the truth and seduce the vulnerable are in real danger (2 Pet. 2:2–3, 14).

Indulge the flesh. Like dumb animals, they live only for their appetites (2 Pet. 2:12).

Its corrupt desires. The desires of the flesh which wage war against the soul (1 Pet. 2:11).

Despise authority. While believers respect and pray for those in authority (1 Tim. 2:2, 1 Pet. 2:13), these mockers speak ill of pastors, politicians, and those with any sort of real authority. They build themselves up by pulling others down, but there is nothing honorable or Christlike about their disdain for others.

Daring or presumptuous. These shameless self-promoters are full of arrogance and pride.

Self-willed. They are self-righteous, unteachable, and egotistical.

They do not tremble. They have no qualms about slandering spiritual beings.

2:11 **Angels who are greater**. The angels of God are mightier and more awesome than loud-mouthed braggarts spouting heresy.

A reviling judgment against them. Angels don't mock and judge each other. If angels refuse to play the judgment game, so should we (Jude 1:9). Judgment is God's business, not ours (Jas. 4:12).

---

2 Peter 2:12–14

[12] But these, like unreasoning animals, born as creatures of instinct
to be captured and killed, reviling where they have no knowledge,
will in the destruction of those creatures also be destroyed, [13] suffering wrong as the wages of doing wrong. They count it a pleasure to
revel in the daytime. They are stains and blemishes, reveling in their
deceptions, as they carouse with you, [14] having eyes full of adultery
that never cease from sin, enticing unstable souls, having a heart
trained in greed, accursed children;

2:12 **Like unreasoning animals**. These false teachers are instinctive, unspiritual creatures living only for their appetites. They have more in common with the beasts than the born-again children of God.

Reviling where they have no knowledge. These scornful critics freely offer opinions about people and subjects they know nothing about. They like to portray themselves as infallible experts, but their sneering, dismissive tone masks their insecurity and ignorance (Jude 1:10).

Destruction... destroyed. The self-destructive way of the flesh leads to corruption and death (Rom. 8:13, Gal. 6:8, 2 Pet. 3:7).

2:13 **Suffering wrong as the wages of doing wrong**. For their wrong doing, these false teachers will reap punishment (2 Pet. 2:9). This punishment will be entirely self-inflicted and utterly contrary to the wishes of God (2 Pet. 3:9). God does not wish for anyone to perish – not even false teachers who malign the truth – and he has gone to extraordinary lengths to deliver us from our destructive choices. But in the end we all reap what we sow, and those who prefer the wages of sin to the free gift of life shall reap death (Rom 6:23).

Revel in the daytime. These ungodly influencers are not secret sinners battling guilt and shame, but daytime sinners flaunting their disgraceful behavior.

They carouse with you making a spectacle of themselves at your love feasts (Jude 1:12). Recall that these false teachers are among you (2 Pet. 2:1). They're in your services, small groups, and social media feeds. They show up at your conferences, concerts, and cookouts.

2:14 **Eyes full of adultery**. Like Balaam of old (see next verse) and Jezebel of Thyatira (Rev. 2:22), these false teachers lead people into idol worship and sexual immorality.

Never cease from sin. They habitually sin because it's in their nature to sin (2 Pet. 2:22). In contrast with the children of God who sometimes stumble, sinners sin because they know no other way to live.

Enticing. The original verb (*deleazo*) means to entrap or bait. They are sheep-stealers, drawing people away from Jesus and to their own rotten ministries.

Unstable souls are those who are in two minds about the gospel (Jas. 1:8). (The original word for unstable (*asteriktos*) means vacillating.) They have heard the gospel and they may have even repented. But since they are not standing firm in the true grace of God (1 Pet. 5:12), they remain susceptible to deception and every wind of doctrine taught by false teachers (Eph. 4:14).

Greed. False teachers are in it for the money (see next verse). They have dollar signs in their eyes. They have no interest in equipping the saints or helping the hurting. They're after the offerings and honorariums. They take but never give.

Accursed children. False teachers are the cursed children of disobedience (Eph. 5:6) and should not be confused with the beloved children of God (Eph. 5:1).

---

2 Peter 2:15–16

[15] forsaking the right way, they have gone astray, having followed
the way of Balaam, the son of Beor, who loved the wages of unrighteousness; [16] but he received a rebuke for his own transgression, for a
mute donkey, speaking with a voice of a man, restrained the madness of the prophet

---

2:15 **Forsaking the right way**. In contrast with believers who are established in the truth (2 Pet. 1:12), false teachers are far from the truth. Like greedy Balaam, they have chosen the wrong path (Num. 22:32).

Gone astray. Going astray is a sign of a restless and unbelieving heart (Heb. 3:18).

The way of Balaam. For a fee paid by the king of Moab, Balaam the prophet enticed the Israelites into idol worship and sexual immorality (Num. 25:1–3, Rev. 2:14). Because of his treachery, Balaam's name became synonymous with greed and deception. In the New Testament, Balaamites were sometimes known as Nicolaitans. The Nicolaitans were libertines who infiltrated the church and introduced destructive heresies (Rev. 2:15).

The wages of unrighteousness. Money. On two occasions Balaam told the messengers of Moab that he could not be bought for any amount, not even a house full of silver and gold (Num. 22:7, 18, 24:13). But somewhere along the way he sold out. Balaam showed Moab how to put stumbling blocks in front of Israel, and for this the Israelites killed him (Num. 31:8, 16, Rev. 2:14).

2:16 **A rebuke**. Balaam's donkey could see what the prophet himself could not see, that the angel of the Lord was opposing him (Num. 22:28–31).

Madness. Insanity. Balaam was mad to think he could harm God's people and get away with it. The same could be said of any false prophet or false teacher.

---

2 Peter 2:17–19

[17] These are springs without water and mists driven by a storm, for
whom the black darkness has been reserved. [18] For speaking out arrogant words of vanity they entice by fleshly desires, by sensuality,
those who barely escape from the ones who live in error, [19] promising
them freedom while they themselves are slaves of corruption; for by
what a man is overcome, by this he is enslaved.

2:17 **Springs without water**. The false teachers who trouble the church are all talk and no action (Pro. 25:14). These time-wasters promise much but deliver little.

Mists driven by a storm. Like clouds carried along by the wind, their teaching is all over the place. One day they say this, the next they say that. Since they are not established in the truth, their teaching is full of contradictions.

Black darkness. Those who close their minds to the light of God's love wander in darkness (1 John 2:11). Although the gospel of grace shines like a beacon calling them home, they prefer to remain outside in the dark and cold.

God patiently waits for the ungodly to repent because he does not want anyone to perish (2 Pet. 3:9). But those who persist in stubborn unbelief eventually cut themselves off from the One who is light. Like wandering stars that drift out of the galaxy, they flicker into blackness and are gone for good (Jude 1:13).

2:18 **Arrogant words of vanity**. These licentious teachers are loudmouths who brag about things they don't understand.

They entice by fleshly desires. Their teaching tickles the ears and appeals to the intellect, but it leaves your spirit unmoved and does not feed your faith.

Sensuality. They seduce the unstable by promoting licentious or immoral lifestyles.

Those who barely escape are the immature and unstable who are susceptible to bad teaching (2 Pet. 2:14). False teachers don't go after mature believers. They go after those unstable souls who are not yet standing firm in the grace of God (2 Pet. 2:14).

The ones who live in error are the false teachers preaching license (see 2 Pet. 2:1).

2:19 **Are slaves of corruption**. Those who preach grace as a license to sin use words like freedom and liberty, while they themselves remain enslaved to sin. On their platforms and profiles they may portray something that looks like freedom. But if you knew their secrets you would see that they are as captive to sin as any sinner.

For by what a man is overcome, by this he is enslaved. These false teachers think they are free but they couldn't stop sinning if they tried (Rom. 6:16). The only remedy for sin is the grace of God that teaches us to deny ungodliness (Tit. 2:11–12). Only Jesus can set us free from the power of sin (John 8:36).

---

2 Peter 2:20–22

[20] For if, after they have escaped the defilements of the world by the knowledge of the Lord and Savior Jesus Christ, they are again entangled in them and are overcome, the last state has become worse for them than the first. [21] For it would be better for them not to have known the way of righteousness, than having known it, to turn away from the holy commandment handed on to them. [22] It has happened to them according to the true proverb, "A dog returns to its own vomit," and, "A sow, after washing, returns to wallowing in the mire."

2:20 **Escaped the defilements of the world**. These false teachers briefly escaped the defilements of the world when they heard the good news. For a moment they saw the open door and the way to freedom. But the message they heard did not profit them because it was not combined with faith (Heb. 4:2). Like the unbelieving Israelites who escaped the defilements of Egypt but fell in the wilderness, they did not enter the Promised Land.

Some use this verse to suggest that Peter is talking about misguided Christians, as if God would destroy his wayward children! The Good Shepherd deals gently with his straying sheep (Heb. 5:2). He rescues them and doesn't condemn them to blackest darkness (2 Pet. 2:17). The context shows that Peter is discussing false teachers who deny the Lord, remain enslaved to sin, and are unspiritual creatures (2 Pet. 2:1, 12, 19). They follow Balaam not Jesus (2 Pet. 2:1, 15).

Knowledge without faith does not equal salvation.

There are those who know and believe the love that God has for us (1 John 4:16), and there are others who know but don't believe. These false teachers heard about the love of God, but they never repented. They hardened their hearts and set themselves up as enemies of God leaving them worse off than before.

The last state has become worse. Those who are lost may be found, but those who have rejected the gospel put themselves in a bad place. It is all but impossible for them to come to the place of repentance (Heb. 6:4–6).

2:21 **Better for them not to have known**. The one who rejects the way of righteousness is worse off because he has hardened his heart to that which could save him. Again, this is not talking about a wayward child of God. Those who have been born again of imperishable seed (1 Pet. 1:23) may stray from time to time, but since they are held in Christ's mighty hand they are eternally secure (John 10:28–29).

The way of righteousness is synonymous with the gospel of grace for the gospel reveals the righteousness that comes from God (Php. 3:9).

The holy commandment is not the gospel (which is an announcement; 1 Pet. 1:12). Nor is it the law of righteousness (which is not based on faith; Rom. 3:12). The holy commandment of God is the command to believe in his Son Jesus Christ (1 John 3:23). These false teachers did not heed this command but turned away from it. They responded to the good news by turning their backs to Jesus.

2:22 **Proverb**. The meaning of the proverb is that false teachers act like sinners because they have not been born again. Having no fellowship with the Lord, they are unable to partake in his divine nature (2 Pet. 1:4).

Dog... sow. The proverb about the dog comes from Prov. 26:11, while the proverb about the sow is not found in the Old Testament. (It may have been a rabbinical proverb or a Greek proverb familiar to first-century listeners.) The point is that dogs act like dogs and pigs act like pigs because it's in their nature to do so. In the same way, sinners act like sinners because they have not been born again. This proverb is not about misguided Christians who occasionally stumble. It's about false teachers who deny the Master, turn away from the gospel, and remain enslaved to sin (2 Pet. 2:1, 19, 21).

---

2 Peter 3

2 Peter 3:1–2

1 This is now, beloved, the second letter I am writing to you in which I am stirring up your sincere mind by way of reminder, 2 that you should remember the words spoken beforehand by the holy prophets and the commandment of the Lord and Savior spoken by your apostles.

3:1 **The second letter**. Since this is Peter's second letter "to you," we can conclude that it went to the same place as his first one, namely to the believers scattered throughout the Roman provinces of Pontus, Galatia, Cappadocia, Asia, and Bithynia (1 Pet. 1:1).

Stirring up. I'm trying to awaken your good and pure minds.

Your sincere mind. Your heart is in the right place and you are established in the truth, but I want to remind you of a few things.

By way of reminder. I want to remind you how to walk in this new life that God has given us (chapter 1), and I want to remind you of what the prophets and apostles said about being ready for the Lord's return (chapter 3).

3:2 **Remember**. To remember the words of the Old Testament prophets, the Lord, and the New Testament apostles is to remember or be mindful of what God has said in scripture. In context, we are to be mindful of what the Bible says about the Lord's final coming (see 2 Pet. 3:4, 10).

The commandment of the Lord. Be ready for the Lord's return (Luke 12:36, 40).

There are several great commands of the Lord in the New Testament. There is the command of God to believe in his Son Jesus Christ (1 John 3:23), and the command of Jesus to, "Love one another, as I have loved you" (John 13:34). But the context indicates that this command has to do with the final coming of the Lord (see 2 Pet. 3:4, 10). It is the Lord's oft-repeated instruction to be ready and waiting for his return

(Matt. 24:42–44, 25:13, Mark 13:33–35, 37, Luke 12:40, 21:36–37, 40).

Apostles. In their epistles the apostles remind us to be ready and eagerly await the return of the Lord (Rom. 8:23, 8:25, 1 Cor. 1:7, 1 Thess. 1:10, Php. 3:20, Jas. 5:7–8, Jude 1:21, Rev. 3:11).

---

2 Peter 3:3–4

3 Know this first of all, that in the last days mockers will come with
their mocking, following after their own lusts, 4 and saying, "Where
is the promise of his coming? For ever since the fathers fell asleep,
all continues just as it was from the beginning of creation."

3:3 **This first of all**. The first thing you need to know about the return of the Lord is that there will be some who don't believe Jesus is coming back at all.

The last days began when Jesus commenced his earthly ministry. Peter believed he was living in the last days (Acts 2:17, 1 Pet. 1:20), as did Paul (2 Tim. 3:1), James (Jas. 5:3) and John (1 John 2:18). We are still living in the last days.

Mockers will come. Last days' mockers are nothing new. In New Testament times there were some who doubted whether the Lord would ever return (see next verse) and others who said he already had (2 Tim. 2:18).

The wrong way to read this scripture is to apply it exclusively to our generation. "We have skeptics and mockers, therefore Jesus is on his way." But Peter's warning covers the entire period of the last days. His warning was for his generation and our generation and every generation until the return of the Lord.

Following after their own lusts. Living without any regard for the things of the Spirit.

3:4 **The promise of his coming**. The Old Testament prophets and Jesus himself all spoke of his future return to earth (e.g., Matt. 16:27, 24:27, 37–39, Luke 17:28–30, John 14:3).

Coming. The original word (*parousia*) is derived from an oriental word used to describe the royal visit of a king or emperor. It is an apt description of the final and glorious return of the Lord.

The fathers fell asleep. Our ancestors died. The prophets and apostles who foretold of the Lord's coming died without seeing the fulfillment of the promise.

All continues. Generations come and go and there is still no sign of the Lord's return. This leads mockers to ask, "Where is this so-called coming of the Lord?"

---

2 Peter 3:5–7

5 For when they maintain this, it escapes their notice that by the word
of God the heavens existed long ago and the earth was formed out
of water and by water, 6 through which the world at that time was
destroyed, being flooded with water. 7 But by his word the present
heavens and earth are being reserved for fire, kept for the day of judgment and destruction of ungodly men.

3:5 **They maintain this**. They mock on purpose. They consciously reject God's word.

It escapes their notice. The mockers seem to forget that the same God who spoke the universe into existence also spoke about judgment and destruction (see 2 Pet. 3:7). We would do well to heed what God has said.

The word of God is powerful, creative, and sustains all things (Gen. 1:3, John 1:1, Heb. 1:3). What God says always comes to pass. When God speaks, we should pay attention. Listen to God and don't heed the mockers.

3:6 **Flooded**. What God made with a word he destroyed with a word (Gen. 6:17).

Many years earlier, Peter had asked Jesus about his future return to earth (Matt. 24:3). The Lord replied that his coming would be like the days of Noah and the days of Lot (Matt. 24:37–39, Luke 17:26–30). From this Peter understood that the Lord's return would be sudden and disruptive like the flood of Noah and the destruction of Sodom.

3:7 **By his word**. The same word that created the earth (verse 5) and destroyed it in a flood (verse 6) will one day burn it with fire (see verse 10).

Reserved for fire. The heavens and the earth will be destroyed by fire and replaced with new versions of each (2 Pet. 3:10, Rev. 21:1).

The Lord often spoke of fire in connection with Judgment Day (Matt. 5:22, 13:42, 50, 18:9, 25:41, Mark 9:43, Luke 12:49, 17:29–30, John 15:6), and Peter develops that fiery theme here. But what does it mean to say the present heavens and earth are reserved for fire?

Those who opt for a preterist interpretation say these prophecies were fulfilled in the Roman destruction of Jerusalem. They note that heaven and earth was a shorthand phrase for the temple, God's heavenly seat on earth. But the context here is Judgment Day and the destruction of the ungodly. In contrast with the fall of Jerusalem, which was preceded by wars and lawlessness (Matt. 24:6, 12), the return of the Lord will occur during a time of peace (Matt. 24:37–38). The former event was well-signposted, but the Lord will return unexpectedly like a thief in the night (2 Pet. 3:10).

Peter is speaking of a destructive end-of-days event. Just as the earth was destroyed by water (see previous verse), it will be destroyed by fire (2 Pet. 3:10). But that does not mean the earth will cease to exist (Ecc. 1:4). Just as the earth survived the flood, we can look forward to a new earth after the fire (2 Pet. 3:13).

The day of judgment; see 2 Pet. 2:9.

Destruction. The original word (*apoleia*), which appears five times in this epistle (twice in 2 Pet. 2:1, 2:3, 3:7, and 3:16), is related to another word (*apollumi*) which means to destroy fully. There is no coming back from this kind of destruction.

Destruction of ungodly men. Those who reject Life reap death. Those who reject the gift of life shall perish in the ultimate or second death (John 5:40, 10:28, Rev 2:11).

There are two outcomes for humanity: eternal life, for those who believe in Jesus, and death for those who don't (John 3:16). These stark outcomes were preached by all the apostles including Paul (Rom. 6:23, 2 Th. 1:8–9), James (Jas. 4:12), John (1 John 3:15, Rev. 11:18, 21:8), and Peter (2 Pet. 2:6, 12). People don't go to hell for their sins, because all our sins were dealt with at the cross (1 Pet. 3:18). But those who reject the Author of Life reject life itself and will be lost forever.

---

2 Peter 3:8–9

[8] But do not let this one fact escape your notice, beloved, that with
the Lord one day is like a thousand years, and a thousand years like
one day. [9] The Lord is not slow about his promise, as some count
slowness, but is patient toward you, not wishing for any to perish
but for all to come to repentance.

3:8 **A thousand years**. God does not measure time the same way we do (Ps. 90:4).

God's schedule is not our schedule and his patience is long. In his eschatological parables, Jesus told stories of masters, noblemen, and bridegrooms being gone a long time (Matt. 24:48, 25:5, 25:19). We need to wait patiently for the Lord's return.

3:9 **His promise** to return; see 2 Pet. 3:4.

Patient; see 2 Pet. 3:15.

Not wishing. God doesn't want anyone to perish yet people perish every day. This shows us that not everything that happens is God's will. Much of the world remains under the influence of the evil one and the powers of darkness (1 John 5:19).

God gave humanity authority over the earth and we opened the door to sin and death. We can't blame God for all the pain and suffering in the world. That's on us. But even though we made a mess of his beautiful creation, our Redeemer is making all things new (see 2 Pet. 3:13).

Perish. God doesn't want anyone to die but desires all to be saved (1 Tim. 2:4). This is why he delays the final Judgment – to give us time to preach the gospel and to give others time to heed it.

Repentance is the ability to receive the truth that sets us free. It's a change of mind that causes us to see as God sees and think as God thinks. Repentance and faith are two sides of the same coin. Like faith, repentance is a response to God's love and grace (Rom. 2:4).

---

2 Peter 3:10–11

10 But the day of the Lord will come like a thief, in which the heavens
will pass away with a roar and the elements will be destroyed with
intense heat, and the earth and its works will be burned up. 11 Since
all these things are to be destroyed in this way, what sort of people
ought you to be in holy conduct and godliness,

3:10 **The day of the Lord** is the day when Jesus will be revealed from heaven with his mighty angels (2 Th. 1:7). This day is also known as the day of judgment (2 Pet. 2:9).

A thief. Jesus is no thief, but he will break into our world in a sudden and thief-like way (Matt. 24:43, 1 Th. 5:2, Rev. 3:3). "Behold, I am coming like a thief" (Rev. 16:15).

The heavens will pass away. From the Lord's own lips, Peter heard that heaven and earth will pass away (Matt. 24:35). The sinful earth passing away we can understand, but why heaven or *the heavens*? Peter is referring to the temple, say some. Yet this is unlikely since the context is the day of the Lord or Judgment Day (2 Pet. 3:7, 12). The word for heavens (*ouranos*) is sometimes translated as sky. It's the same word John uses when he says the sky will vanish like a rolled-up scroll (Rev. 6:14; see also Is. 34:4). Perhaps Peter is saying our polluted atmosphere will be replaced with something new. Just as the land will be made new, so too the sky and the air that we breathe will be replaced, reset, or refreshed in some way.

The elements will be destroyed. The original word for elements (*stoicheion*) can mean physical elements, but it can also refer to the basic principles or rules for survival in a world captive to sin (Gal. 4:3). The old world order, which is subject to principalities and powers, will be destroyed or melted or dissolved with intense heat (2 Pet. 3:12). Things which are temporal and cursed will be replaced by things which are eternal and blessed.

The earth... burned up. The land that was stained by sin will be scoured by fire and made new.

Note that it is *the earth* that is burned up, not *the world*. Peter has already mentioned how "the world," "the ancient world," and "the world of the ungodly" was destroyed by a flood (2 Pet. 2:5, 3:6), but here he uses a different word; not *kosmos*, which means world, but *ge*, which is sometimes translated as land or ground (e.g., Matt. 27:45). First Adam cursed the ground with his disobedience (Gen. 3:17), but Last Adam blessed the earth with his obedience.

God's wonderful creation is going to be liberated from its bondage to decay (Rom. 8:20–21). The world will not be obliterated in a firestorm for "the earth remains forever" (Ecc. 1:4). But those parts of the earth that have been harmed by sin will be made new (Rev. 21:5). How this plays out is yet to be seen, but we can be confident that the world that God gave us will be transformed into a beautiful and eternal home. It will be even better than Eden because the ruler of the new earth will not be fallen Adam but Jesus himself (Rev. 21:3).

3:11 **All these things**. The heavens, earth, the elements (see previous verse) and the ungodly will be destroyed (2 Pet. 3:7).

Destroyed in this way. By fire.
Holy conduct and godliness. When we who are holy conduct ourselves in holiness, we provide the world with a prophetic picture of the new world to come.

---

2 Peter 3:12–13

[12] looking for and hastening the coming of the day of God, because of which the heavens will be destroyed by burning, and the elements will melt with intense heat! [13] But according to his promise we are looking for new heavens and a new earth, in which righteousness dwells.

3:12 **Hastening**. We hasten the Lord's return by living holy lives that point people to our holy Father.
Those who insist that Peter's prophecies of fiery destruction were fulfilled when the Romans burned Jerusalem have a difficult time explaining this verse. "New Testament believers hastened the coming of the Lord by crying out to God for justice, and their prayers were answered when the Romans slaughtered the Jews." Such an interpretation is at odds with the evidence (this letter was sent to Christians who lived nowhere near Judea) and contrary to the heart of a gracious and forgiving God (2 Pet. 3:9).
The day of God or the day of the Lord is also known as the day of judgment; see 2 Pet. 2:9.
Destroyed by burning; see 2 Pet. 3:7.
Elements; see 2 Pet. 3:10.

3:13 **His promise** of a new heaven and earth (e.g., Is. 65:17, 66:22, Acts 3:21, Rom. 8:19–21, Rev. 21:1, 5).
We are looking. Every believer is looking forward to the day when this broken and cursed world will be made new. On that day there will be no more death, mourning, crying, or pain, for the former things will have passed away (Rev. 21:4).

New heaven and a new earth. The eternal age, where God dwells with humanity on earth. In the imagery of Revelation, the new heaven and earth correspond to the City of God, a.k.a., the new Jerusalem or the church. There is a wonderful symmetry here. Just as the temple of Jerusalem was known as heaven and earth in the old covenant, in the new covenant the church represents the new heaven and earth (Rev. 21:1). But the church is just the trailer, not the movie.

On the Mount of Transfiguration, Peter got a preview of Christ's kingly glory (2 Pet. 1:16). In the same way, the church presents the world with a glimpse of the new world to come (Eph. 3:10). One day God will bring an end to all those things that oppose his good will and heaven and earth will be made new. It is a day to look forward to (see next verse).

Righteousness dwells. The present world is marred by sin, but the new earth will be the home of righteousness. In that blessed realm there will be no more sorrow or suffering or harm or death (Is. 65:25, Rev. 21:4, 27).

---

2 Peter 3:14–15

14 Therefore, beloved, since you look for these things, be diligent to
be found by him in peace, spotless and blameless, 15 and regard the
patience of our Lord as salvation; just as also our beloved brother
Paul, according to the wisdom given him, wrote to you,

3:14 **You look for these things**. As believers we are looking forward to the day when the Lord will return and wipe away every tear and make all things new (Rev. 21:4).

Be diligent. Make this a priority; see 2 Pet. 1:10.

Peace comes from having a mind submitted to the Spirit and a heart that has found its rest in the Lord (Is. 26:3, Rom. 8:6, Php. 4:7).

Spotless and blameless. Since Jesus makes us spotless and blameless, the call to be found spotless and blameless is a call to be who we are in Christ. In Christ you are holy, so be holy and have nothing to do with the destructive desires of the flesh (1 Pet. 1:15).

3:15 **Patience**. We may be impatient for the Lord's return, but he is in no hurry at all. Time is on his side and the longer he waits, the bigger his family grows. Like a mustard seed that grows into a great tree, God's kingdom is growing every day (Matt. 13:32).

Salvation. God's patience means more people get saved (2 Pet. 3:9).

Our beloved brother Paul. The apostle Paul rebuked Peter for withdrawing from the Gentiles and then wrote about Peter's shameful behavior in a letter (Gal. 2:11–12). To his eternal credit, Peter harbored no ill will towards Paul, but called him a beloved brother. Truly, Peter had a teachable spirit and a heart inclined towards grace.

The wisdom given to him. Paul, who was well known to the churches in the regions around Asia and Galatia, had made similar claims regarding the patience of the Lord (e.g., Rom. 2:4, 9:22, Heb. 10:36).

Wrote to you. Which letters from Paul is Peter referring to? Given his audience, he could be referring to Paul's letters to the Galatians (who lived in Galatia), the Ephesians and the Colossians (who lived in Asia).

---

2 Peter 3:16–18

16 as also in all his letters, speaking in them of these things, in which are some things hard to understand, which the untaught and unstable distort, as they do also the rest of the Scriptures, to their own destruction. 17 You therefore, beloved, knowing this beforehand, be on your guard so that you are not carried away by the error of unprincipled men and fall from your own steadfastness, 18 but grow in the grace and knowledge of our Lord and Savior Jesus Christ. To him be the glory, both now and to the day of eternity. Amen.

3:16 **All his letters**. Peter wrote his second letter shortly before his execution in AD64 (see 2 Pet. 1:14). At that time, Paul's letters had been circulating for ten years or more and they were well known in the early church. Since Peter had read *all* of Paul's letters, we might conclude that Paul had died and was no longer writing.

These things. These questions about the final return of the Lord.

Hard to understand. Peter is not referring to the gospel of grace, which he understood perfectly (1 Pet. 1:13, 5:12). The context suggests he is referring to those parts of Paul's eschatological teachings which are hard to understand and open to misinterpretation (e.g., the apostasy and the man of lawlessness; see 2 Th. 2:1–8).

The untaught and unstable distort. False teachers who don't know what they are talking about hijack Paul's words to say things Paul never said. This is particularly true when it comes to the man of lawlessness (2 Th. 2:3).

This passage is not talking about confused or uneducated Christians. Peter is pointing back to the villains of the previous chapter. He's talking about wolves in sheep's clothing who infiltrate the church to attack the flock.

The rest of the Scriptures. Peter considers Paul's letters as equal in authority to the Old Testament.

We are familiar with Paul's letters because they are in the Bible. But in the first century, his letters were little more than bits of parchment passed around the churches. Yet even then they were recognized as divinely inspired and *scriptural*.

To their own destruction. Their downfall is their own fault and not God's punishment.

3:17 **Be on your guard**. Watch what you hear and read. Listen to unstable teachers and you may become unstable yourself.

Unprincipled or unstable teachers are those who distort the teachings of the New Testament (see previous verse).

Fall from your own steadfastness. Listening to false teachers who mishandle the gospel of grace can leave you feeling anxious and insecure. So don't listen to them, but grow in the grace and knowledge of Jesus instead (see next verse).

3:18 **Grow**. We are exhorted to grow in grace and we do this by growing in our revelation knowledge of Jesus Christ. As we allow the Holy Spirit to reveal good things to us about the Lord, we grow in grace.

Believers who have little understanding of God's grace remain immature and susceptible to bad teaching (2 Pet. 2:14). The remedy is not to run after the latest teaching but to crave the pure milk of the word so that you may grow (1 Pet. 2:2). Jesus is the Living Word and the Bread of Life, and the more we feed on him the more we grow.

Grace; see 1 Pet. 5:5.

Savior Jesus. Peter ends his epistle the way he started it, by declaring that Jesus is equal with God (2 Pet. 1:1). Jesus is the Savior and God is our Savior (Jude 1:25). Truly the Father and the Son are One (John 10:30).

Glory; see 2 Pet. 1:3.

The day of eternity is the day eternity begins. It is Judgment Day, or the day of the Lord when Jesus is revealed from heaven (2 Pet. 2:9).

Amen. So be it.

Index

Note: Key entries are in bold.

A Message from the Author

If you enjoyed reading *The Grace Bible: 1–2 Peter*, would you mind posting a short customer review on Amazon or social media (#thegracebible)? Doing so will help others hear the good news of God's grace. Thank you.

New instalments and new formats in *The Grace Bible* series will be available soon. Sign up for notifications at thegracebible.com and be the first to know.

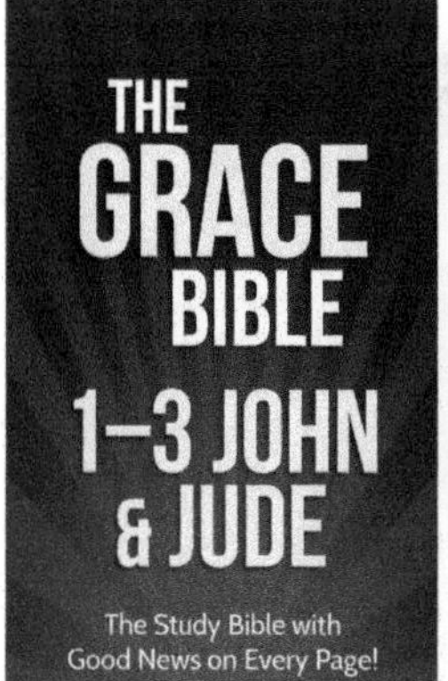

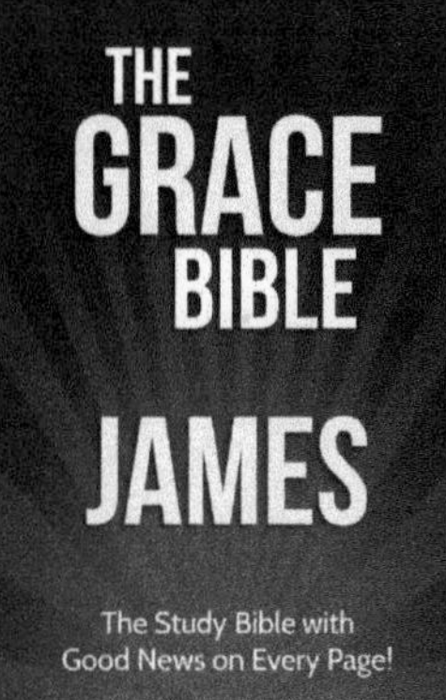

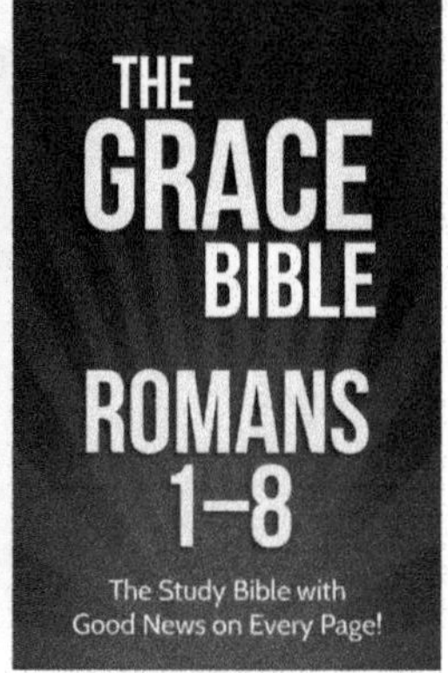

Printed in the USA
CPSIA information can be obtained
at www.ICGtesting.com
LVHW061025120823
755047LV00042B/897